IAN FLEMING

The Spy Who Came In with the Gold

Books by HENRY A. ZEIGER

IAN FLEMING

The Spy Who Came In with the Gold

by HENRY A. ZEIGER

DUELL, SLOAN AND PEARCE   •   New York

Second printing, February, 1966

DUELL, SLOAN & PEARCE
AFFILIATE OF
MEREDITH PRESS

Library of Congress Catalog Card Number: 65-26809

MANUFACTURED IN THE UNITED STATES OF AMERICA FOR MEREDITH PRESS

VAN REES PRESS   •   NEW YORK

The author would like to acknowledge the substantial assistance of James A. Bryans, who has very good ideas and knows how to spell, and of Gail Kennedy, who did much of the research for this book.

Contents

IAN FLEMING

The Spy Who Came In with the Gold

CHAPTER

1

The First Hero

LISBON in 1941 was a hotbed of international intrigue. Refugees, black marketeers, businessmen with shady deals in wolfram, and every variety of agent and double agent flocked to the city. The young assistant to the Director of Naval Intelligence, Ian Fleming, recognized many suspect faces as he looked around the casino at Estoril.

He paid particular attention to the *chemin de fer* table, for gathered there were several of the leading members of German Intelligence, playing a high-stakes game.

"Look," he said to his chief, Admiral John Godfrey, pointing to the Germans, "what a wonderful chance for a little useful mischief."

"What do you mean?" the Admiral asked.

"I've been watching them. I'm sure we can take them at chemmy. That way we can run our own operations in Lisbon on German money."

"I don't play the game," the Admiral replied, "but if you think you can do something, by all means go ahead."

Fleming had fifty pounds travel money in his pocket and he was an experienced gambler. The Germans were making the bank at *chemin de fer,* and in this game the odds only slightly favor the banker. Fleming thought that his own experience would more than offset the slight edge that the Germans would have. Of course, he knew he would also have to be lucky.

He wasn't. A half hour later he rejoined Godfrey, having dropped his entire stake, and shamefacedly requested additional travel funds. Godfrey handed them to him when they were both safely seated on the Clipper for Washington, far removed from the distractions of *chemin de fer.*

Years later, Ian Fleming used this situation as the basis for the central incident of his first novel, *Casino Royale.* In the novel the British agent, James Bond, decisively defeats the Communist agent, Le Chiffre, at a game of *chemin de fer,* thereby putting an end to his evil machinations. As is so often the case, fiction turned out much, much better than real life ever had.

Ian Fleming was the most fantastically successful novelist (in commercial terms) of the past decade. What had been intended by Fleming as a mild diversion from the distractions of marriage at the age of forty-three, eventually turned into a gold-plated industry, and he sold a 51 per cent share of his creation in 1964 for $280,000. A book that Fleming was sure no one would want to publish—and that he was even reluctant to acknowledge the existence of—led to a series of twelve novels with a sale of over thirty million copies in the United States and England alone, to three of the more profitable films of the era, and even to a line of 007 toiletries marketed by the Colgate-Palmolive Company.

Whatever the final literary judgment as to the value of Fleming's novels, there is no question that in James Bond he succeeded in creating a hero with enormous popular appeal. Fleming fitted together a certain combination of ingredients which was unique, and though he had no very high opinion of his creation and no very serious purpose in mind, he somehow drew from his imagination a character that pleasantly corresponded to the daydreams of his readers.

Like all writers, no matter what their intentions (and after the first book Fleming deliberately cultivated commercial success), Fleming used his past life as it had survived in his memory for the stuff on which his imagination fed. Of course, most of his novels are not autobiographical, and it was rarely the case that an incident like the one in the casino at Estoril fitted itself to the requirements of suspense with so little adaptation. Still, there were certain patterns in his life, certain attitudes and feelings, which persist in his fiction and which can be traced in the known events of his biography. In particular, Ian Fleming always required a hero, and James Bond is a summing up of a number of real men by whom Fleming was fascinated.

Ian Fleming's first hero, it is safe to say, was his father, who died in World War I, when Ian was only eight. Ian probably had only slight personal memories of his father, Major Valentine Fleming, but of course a boy whose father is not present has all the more need and opportunity to idealize him. In Ian Fleming's case he was on fairly safe ground, for Major Valentine Fleming, who was posthumously awarded the D.S.O., was the genuine article. In 1927 a history of Major Fleming's regiment, the Oxfordshire Hussars, was published by one of the former officers of the regiment, Lieutenant Keith Falconer. If there is one officer in the regiment who emerges from this account as always being in the right place in time to do the right thing, it is Major Valentine Fleming. It is fairly certain that Ian Fleming knew this history, in which the record of his father's gallantry plays so conspicuous a part.

Edwardian England, Valentine Fleming's England, England before the Great War, was certainly a very good thing for some people, and among those people were the Flemings. Ian's paternal grandfather, Robert Fleming, was a private banker and a sometime associate of J. P. Morgan. From the size of Valentine Fleming's estate, it can be surmised that Robert Fleming was a very successful man and that his success gave his son, Valentine, the chance to lead an extremely comfortable life in the style of an English country gentleman of the best type.

For while Valentine Fleming was among those lucky people in Edwardian England who took it for granted that the world was a pleasant place to live in, he was not a man of leisure. From *Who's Who* (in England) we learn that he attended Eton, where he rowed on the Eton Eight, and then went on to Magdalen College at Oxford, from which he graduated in 1905 with Honours in History. He was called to the Bar of the Inner Temple in 1907 and became a partner in his father's firm of bankers, Robert Fleming and Company.

Valentine Fleming married Evelyn B. St. C. Rose, reportedly one of the most beautiful women in England, and set up housekeeping in Oxfordshire while also maintaining a residence in London. He was an enthusiastic hunter and listed his recreations for *Who's Who* as "deer stalking, salmon fishing, fox hunting," adding that he kept "a pack of Basset hounds."

Sport was an important part of his life, as it was to be for his sons, and Valentine won the Ladies' Plate at Henley in 1904, was in the finals of the Visitor's Cup, and at Oxford rowed for the University Eight.

Peter Fleming, Ian's brother, remembers his grandfather's country house as being "unmanageably capacious." It contained a gun room, and some idea of the style of life there can be gathered from Peter's comments on this room in an essay called "My Aunt's Rhinoceros." He wrote: "I had always liked the gun room, which was smaller and more habitable than the other rather palatial apartments on the ground floor. . . . To it one's earliest dancing partners, limping slightly, had been glad to carry out a planned withdrawal from the Charleston. In it one had worked for examinations, occasionally pontificated, written one's first book." This house was sufficiently large and unmanageable after World War II's emancipation of domestic servants to have been turned into a convalescent home run by the Ministry of Health.

In the days before the Great War, however, there was no servant shortage, and particularly large country houses were staffed by as many as fifty servants, while the masters busied themselves with the sports of the field and the delights of the table. Breakfast in the days of Ian Fleming's

father was a banquet, and Lady Cynthia Asquith recalled:
"Most households were cheerfully resigned to breakfast . . .
going on till half past ten or so, and the little blue flames
under the array of lidded, silver chafing-dishes kept piping
hot the crisp, curly bacon, eggs (poached, boiled and fried),
mounds of damp kedgeree (made with salmon), haddocks
swimming in melted butter, sputtering sausages and ruddily
exuding kidneys. First, the young men of the party would
line themselves with porridge immersed in thick yellow
cream. Next they would pile some of the contents of nearly
each hot dish on to their plates. This course consumed,
they would ram down scones, thickly buttered and topped
with home-made jam, marmalade or honey. Fruit from the
walls, nets or hothouses of the kitchen garden wound up
this minor meal."

It is worth emphasizing such aspects of the life of this
time, for even to such disenchanted spirits as John Osborne,
the Edwardian Age has since appeared to be a Paradise
Lost. Fleming's family actually shared the benefits of the
paradise, and James Bond's later role as a connoisseur of
the fine physical things of life owes something to this ideal
of the English gentry as conspicuous consumers. Also, a
great deal of Fleming's (and others') animus against the
paltry aspects of existence in the era of the Cold War must
derive from a feeling that they have lost their upper-middle-
class inheritance of servants, foxes, gun rooms and large
breakfasts.

But if Valentine Fleming believed in masters and servants, there is every suggestion that he did not feel that the
obligations and duties were all on the side of the lower
orders. On January 25, 1907, *The Times* of London carried

the announcement that "Mr. Valentine Fleming of Joyce
Grove, Nettlebed, has been chosen as the prospective Conservative candidate for South Oxfordshire in place of Sir
Robert Hermon-Hodge who has refused to stand again.
[Sir Robert had taken a beating in the Liberal sweep of
1906.] Mr. Fleming will address a series of meetings in the
division next week."

Valentine Fleming, from the little that can be learned of
his political career in the columns of *The Times,* had the
usual ideas of his party and his class. On May 25, 1908,
The Times reported that at a meeting of the South Oxfordshire Conservative and Unionist Association, "Mr. Fleming,
in responding to the toast of the 'Conservative Cause' criticized the various Government departments and said that
there was an increasing feeling of disgust in the country at
the policy and methods of the present Government. Refer-
ring to old-age pensions, he said that, while statistics showed
that the majority of artisans and other workers succumbed
at 54 or 56 years of age, they were offered the inducement
of pensions at 70, from which the thrifty person would be
debarred and in which the careless spendthrift, if he lived
so long, would participate. The measure was a blow at thrift
and a distinct encouragement of improvidence. The man
who saved an income of 10 shillings per week got nothing;
the man who spent all got 5 shillings per week." In other
words, these pensions were on the one hand a fraud, for
most people didn't live to be 70, and on the other hand
they rewarded the unworthy. (If the sentiment sounds familiar, it is because Goldwater Republicans were still saying
the same thing in 1964.) It must be remembered that the
Liberal pension of 1907 was in its time a rather startling

measure; however, Winston Churchill, who knew Valentine Fleming well and came from a very similar background, was among those leading support for this measure in the House of Commons.

In the election of 1910 Valentine Fleming carried the South Oxfordshire constituency for the Conservatives by a margin of 1603 votes. (In the previous election the Liberals had won by 512.) In the House he did not play a conspicuous part in the great debates of the day, for he was only twenty-eight when he took office. He did speak on the subject of abolishing the absolute veto of the House of Lords and accused the Liberals of "giving way to an extreme section of their party." *The Times* reported that "he noticed that some unsuccessful Radical candidates at the General Election ascribed their defeat in statements to the *Daily News* to wholesale bribery, or, in other words to 'Beer, bribery and bullying.' What a comment upon the electoral system. . . . This is a potent argument in favor of the Second Chamber."

But the veto of the House of Lords was abolished, the pension was passed, as was a National Insurance Bill, and it was known that the Liberals had a number of other schemes ready for the restructuring of society. Lloyd George and the Liberals were trying to change the England of fox hunts and country houses. Lloyd George said, "Who ordained that a few should have the land of Britain as a perquisite? Who made ten thousand people owners of the soil and the rest of us trespassers on the land of our birth? Who is responsible for the scheme of things whereby one man is engaged through life in grinding labour to win a bare and precarious subsistence . . . and another man who does not toil receives every hour of the day, every hour of the night, whilst he slumbers, more than his poor neighbour receives in a whole year of toil?"

These were bitter words and the feelings they produced in those under attack were also bitter. The paradise of Edwardian England was threatened, and after a few years of fighting a losing battle, *The Times* noted in 1913 that "Mr. Valentine Fleming has intimated his intention of retiring at the end of the present Parliament."

While he was a Member of Parliament, Valentine Fleming spoke on several occasions in debates concerning the organization of the Territorial Forces. He himself was an officer in the Oxfordshire Hussars. The Territorial Forces (or Yeomanry Regiments, as they were also known) were the equivalent of our own National Guard. The officers and men all came from the same district, though there were a number of distinctively Edwardian touches to the organization of these regiments.

For instance, around the turn of the century, as Mr. Keith Falconer notes in his *The History of the Oxfordshire Hussars in the Great War,* "in many cases the troop leader was himself the landlord of all his troopers, or at any rate belonged to the family which for generations had lived in the district from which the men were recruited." The training these regiments received was apt to be informal and for the officers, at least, seems to have been mainly a slightly different kind of country weekend. We read that after the South African War, "annual training was increased to 14 days and took place under canvas in many of the beautiful parks of the country, which were generously lent by their owners."

Winston Churchill, then First Lord of the Admiralty, was also an officer in the regiment and on another occasion "took the Henley and Woodstock Squadrons to Portsmouth, where they were shown the latest Dreadnoughts and dockyards."

In the days immediately preceding World War I, Mr. Desmond Chapman-Huson had some contact with a Yeomanry regiment in Wiltshire which was very similar in composition to the Oxfordshire Hussars. He later recalled those days:

"That summer passed beautifully, as do all Wiltshire summers, good or bad. The Royal Wiltshire Yeomanry were camped near Pythouse in Jack Benett-Stanford's Park. We called on the Officer's Mess and, on the following Sunday, several young subalterns came to return the call and stayed to tea. . . . I liked these agreeable young men as, a few days later, we sat watching their sports, admired their horsemanship, their athletic prowess, their smart blue uniforms with white facings, silver chain shoulderstraps and Royal Red distinctions.

"Officers, non-commissioned officers and men were friends and neighbours and, so to speak, hereditary members of the Regiment. All the officers, and the majority of the men, brought and rode their own horses."

At the outbreak of World War I the Oxfordshire Hussars were called into active service. Keith Falconer remarks, "On the morning of Tuesday, 4th August 1914, the great majority [of the Regiment] would probably have been found at work on the farm."

"The officers of the yeomanry," he states, "were drawn from the landowners and country gentlemen of the district." A footnote provides us with additional information: "Colonel Dugdale was a cloth manufacturer, Major Fiennes and Captain [Valentine] Fleming members of Parliament, Major Churchill [Winston's brother] a stockbroker, Major Nicholl a solicitor, Captain Scott a barrister, Captain Molloy a King's messenger, Lieutenant Fleming [Phillip Fleming, Valentine's brother] a banker, Lieutenant Hutchinson Bursar of Christ Church."

The Oxfordshire Hussars, as their name indicates, were a cavalry regiment. They had been trained in the tactics in vogue in the late 19th century, which proved to be of no possible use to them during the war they actually fought. The attitude both officers and men had to their duties in the days before the war may be summarized by an anecdote. During the annual training, the command of one lieutenant executed a maneuver in a particularly excruciating fashion, whereupon the brigade commander icily inquired whether the lieutenant considered himself a soldier, only to be told, "Good Lord, no, sir. I'm a stockbroker."

After a short period of muddling around in England, the regiment quickly found themselves in the midst of a very real war. They fought in the first battle of Ypres and their role was summarized by Lord French in his book *1914:* "I must add a few words as to the fine part played in the fighting of 1st November by the Oxfordshire Hussars and the London Scottish. They were the first Territorial troops who fought in the war.

"After disembarking at Dunkirk the Oxfordshire Hussars took part in the important operations connected with the Belgian retreat from Antwerp, and rendered most valuable aid in the defense of the Wytschaete-Messines Ridge when that piece of ground was held with such marvellous tenacity by the Cavalry division against overwhelming odds."

At the battle of Ypres, Valentine Fleming was second-in-command of C Squadron, and his brother, Phillip, commanded the 1st Troop in the same squadron. At Messines, the regiment first made contact with the Germans on October 31, 1914, when "a few Germans could be seen running from a little spinney towards a farm building and Captain Fleming and one or two of the men tried to pick them off with a rifle as they crossed the open."

On November 3, with his squadron in reserve and A squadron being heavily shelled, "Captain Valentine Fleming with great gallantry came up from behind to ascertain how the squadron was getting on and [to inquire] if more ammunition was required."

The Oxfordshire Hussars got off lightly at Ypres, but soon returned to the trenches. "About the middle of the morning of Friday, 20th November [1914], Private N. Harcourt, C Squadron, was hit rather badly through the shoulder. Captain Valentine Fleming at once went along to him, had him bandaged up and though it was of course daylight and they were in full view of the enemy, Captain Fleming, helped by Sergeant Hodelinott, carried the man back to the dressing station. It was freezing cold, and if the man had been left in the trench till dark, he might have died of exposure."

Ypres was a bloody affair. There were 50,000 casualties in the Expeditionary Force. The troops who went to France in the early days of the war were, according to C. E. Montague, "men of handsome and boundless illusions." "Each of them quite seriously thought of himself as a molecule in the body of a nation that was really, and not just figura-

tively, 'straining every nerve' to discharge an obligation of
honour. . . . All the air was ringing with rousing assurances.
France to be saved, Belgium righted, freedom and civiliza-
tion re-won, a sour, soiled, crooked old world to be rid of
bullies and crooks and reclaimed for straightness, decency,
good-nature, the ways of common men dealing with common men." Ypres began the dissolution of these notions.

After this early period in the trenches, the Oxfordshire
Hussars were retrained as cavalry and reserved by the General Staff to exploit a breakthrough in the German position.
The idea was that the infantry would open up a breach and
that the cavalry would then "shoot the gap." It was a nice,
simple idea which completely ignored the actual conditions
of trench warfare on the Western Front. By the summer of
1915 the troops had realized this. As Keith Falconer put it,
"To them [the Oxfordshire Hussars] the prospect of open
warfare seemed infinitely more remote now than it did in
October, 1914, and every visit to the trenches confirmed
this impression. It is true that a mysterious operation described as 'going through the gap' was sometimes mentioned, generally in a spirit of rather incredulous levity."
As was usually the case in this war, the men at the front
had a much better idea of the tactics required than the staff,
and a gap never developed through which the cavalry could
shoot.

For the Oxfordshire Hussars the war developed into a
series of training exercises which never were of any practical value, interrupted by short stretches of duty in the
trenches as infantry and periods waiting on horseback for
the mythical gap to develop. The gap was always anticipated at the beginning of any major battle. "The battle of

the Somme began on the 1st July [1916], but after the first day or two the news became less and less hopeful, and the gap preparations finally degenerated into a resumption of training."

Valentine Fleming was promoted to major on December 1, 1914, and took command of C Squadron. He continued in this post until his death, except for a brief period as second-in-command of the regiment. Whatever his private views of the conduct of the war, he believed in keeping himself and his men in the best of condition. Keith Falconer writes: "In C Squadron Major V. Fleming was always an effective and assiduous runner. On the most unlikely occasions in France he was to be found running to keep himself fit—and inducing rather hesitating brother officers to do the same."

In March, 1915, "Major Fleming got up a sort of *concours hippique* against a squadron of the 12th Lancers, and C Squadron distinguished itself by beating the regulars. . . . Mention must be made of the famous night attack which C Squadron did for the benefit of General Bingham and various other generals. . . . It was a huge success chiefly owing to the trouble and thoroughness with which Major Fleming had arranged everything. . . .

"The Brigadier was especially keen on wood-fighting, and each squadron in turn was called on to carry out a practice attack in the neighbouring Fôret de Nieppe. When C Squadron's turn came, Major Fleming had all the men drawn up in front of General Bingham and proceeded to give a most Napoleonic lecture on wood-fighting which greatly impressed the Brigadier; no one could carry off these things more brilliantly than the member for South Oxfordshire."

Major Fleming always stood by his men. In November, 1916, his squadron drew some very bad billets at La Neuville and spent six days with their horses in the open "until the persistent efforts of Major V. Fleming practically forced Brigade Headquarters to give the Regiment the village of Le Ponchel."

Major Fleming continued to distinguish himself. On January 7, 1917, the Brigade supplied a "pioneer battalion"— a labor detail—under his command. "The only noteworthy incident was a wagonload of shells catching fire and the contents exploding. No record remains of what actually happened, but Major Fleming was specially thanked in Corps Orders for his work at the time."

During periods of training, the war had its lighter moments for the regiment. Keith Falconer records: "The Queen's Own Oxfordshire Hussars was the first regiment to play polo in France." When they first went on leave some of the officers brought back harriers and beagles and chased hares with them until the French farmers objected. Until 1915 some of the officers had their own motor cars in the rear areas, which proved useful in hauling items of nonstandard equipment, like Major Fleming's gramophone. The regiment seems to have retained its civilian's contempt for the military mind, for after one inspection an officer noted with amazement: "The Division Commander didn't say anything stupid all day."

In May, 1917, Valentine Fleming was granted special Parliamentary leave and returned to London for about 10 days. He rejoined the regiment at Hamelet, where they were about to take over the Gillemont Farm area. His squadron was scheduled to go forward first, with D in support and A in reserve. They were scheduled to hold the farm for five days and then to be relieved by A Squadron. After the first night in billets, Major Fleming and another officer went on to Gillemont Farm and inspected the position, and they "came back looking much more serious than when they started."

This last incident in Major Fleming's life is narrated in great detail in Keith Falconer's book and gives a very good idea of the kind of officer Valentine Fleming was. On May 16, C Squadron moved up and took over the support position. The next day Major Fleming again went forward to have a look at Gillemont Farm. Keith Falconer describes the position: "To begin with there was no continuous line at all, such as we had been accustomed to on all our previous excursions to the trenches. . . . Here there was only a chain of posts and entrenched positions, separated from one another by fairly considerable stretches of open ground. These gaps in the line were patrolled at night, but there was nothing to prevent substantial bodies of troops coming through and cutting off one or more of our posts. . . ."

Gillemont Farm was a "rather isolated tactical post in the outpost line, and a 'dangerous post.' " The Germans had cover behind a steep slope. From that position they could accurately observe every movement "until one reached the communication trench leading from the road to the farm." The farm itself had been much fought over. "The buildings were all in ruins now, and formed the no-man's-land between us and the enemy, in which listening posts and patrols crawled breathlessly and stealthily in the night watches."

Keith Falconer continues: "The existing situation at Gillemont Farm at the time of C Squadron's arrival was that on several occasions the Hun had raided the place, and on each occasion he had succeeded in getting in. The probability was that he would try again, but one thing was certain—that Major Fleming would never let his squadron be turned out of the position. Friends who saw him on his return from his preliminary tour of inspection observed that he looked unusually grave and serious, and it was evident that he foresaw a hard time ahead."

C Squadron went forward late on the night of May 17th. The same night Major Fleming carried out a personal reconnaissance of the ground in front of the position and sent back a situation report: "At 4 A.M. I went out with a sergeant and found the ruins of the Farm quite clear of the enemy. I was able to get far enough down the sunken road leading to Bony to see the enemy working on a continuation of the line observed by Lieutenant Worsley. Owing to the dim light I cannot guarantee that this line is wired throughout, but parts of it were. Owing to being fired upon by an enemy sentry I returned to the Farm buildings and worked down the southern side, and was able to observe what was *apparently* the end of the wired portion of the enemy line behind Gillemont Farm. I saw three enemy in a wired sap at the extreme S. end of the line."

The next few days were spent improving the Squadron's position: "deepening saps to posts, strengthening posts, strengthening parapets, wiring, improvement of fire steps, draining communication trenches, improving squadron headquarters, etc." Most of the work was done at night and was interrupted by the movement of enemy troops and by shell fire. The volume of enemy activity continually increased and

Keith Falconer, reviewing Major Fleming's reports after the war, felt "an unexpressed foreboding of attack."

At 1 A.M. on Sunday, May 20th, Major Fleming replied to an inquiry from headquarters by reporting, "My squadron holds its locality." At 2:30 A.M. he sent back a situation report: "All quiet 3 P.M.—7 P.M. Thence to 9 P.M. gradually increasing shelling by heavy enemy H.E.s thickened towards 9 P.M. by trench mortars and gas shells."

Keith Falconer continues: "This was the last message received from Major Fleming.

"Suddenly the storm broke. Almost exactly at 3 A.M. the Germans began a hurricane bombardment of Gillemont Farm with heavy guns and trench mortars, which lasted about half an hour. Presumably most of the squadron took what shelter they could in the rather inadequate trenches, and practically all we know of this period is that at some moment—the exact time is not known—Major Fleming was going up from his squadron headquarters to the right-hand sector of the line and that about ten yards from the front line he probably met Silvertop (another officer), and a shell landed on the trench and killed them both instantaneously."

Shortly after his death the shelling stopped and the Germans attacked in force. Previously, the practice had been not to hold the farm against such attacks, but this time the squadron remained in position, following Major Fleming's orders, and the Germans were repelled with heavy losses.

Keith Falconer wrote of Valentine Fleming:

No greater blow could have befallen the Regiment than the death of Major Fleming. Beloved by his many friends, worshipped by his squadron, admired and repected by all, he was a most gallant officer, a born leader of men. Deriving authority from his own ability and merit, being also a man of notable courage, he was able to control men freely by strength of character and personal example rather than by force of military discipline. Having everything at home to make life good, he set it aside utterly to serve his country. For he was by no means one of those, happy in their generation, who love fighting for fighting's sake; to him it was all thoroughly distasteful, and in quiet times behind the line he was never tired of descanting on the utter weariness of the whole thing. And yet he might so easily, and with perfect justification, have obtained a responsible staff appointment, in which he would not only have been reasonably safe and comfortable, but would also have done good and valuable work for the country. For his intellectual abilities were considerable, well above those of many staff officers. But that was not his way; he recognized the importance of staff work, and the need of able men to do it well. Only it just wasn't his ideal of service.

He was noted also for a complete understanding of his duty, and for great energy and self-discipline in its performance. He never spared himself, and he expected the same of others. It was typical of him that after a long day reconnoitring a position, or doing some other job, he would return to billets thoroughly tired and immediately set to work studying plans for the morrow, writing orders, interviewing the sergeant-major, or inspecting billets, stables, etc. Thoroughness was his motto in all things, and he never left to others work that he could possibly do himself. Witness one of the last exploits of his life, the already-mentioned reconnaissance in front of his position at Gillemont Farm. Nine squadron leaders out of ten would have sent a subaltern or sergeant to do the patrol and report, and no one would have thought the worse of them for doing so. Major Fleming went himself.

He did not always suffer fools gladly, and could not endure the slacker, of whom there were few in his squadron; they generally found it convenient to change their habits.

The Regiment lost in Val Fleming not only a brave and capable officer but also a character of singular charm and attraction.

Those who knew him best perhaps remember him chiefly as the
staunchest and truest of friends, the gayest and brightest of com-
rades; they recall the athletic figure with the long, quick stride
and the keen eager face, the laughter and talk full of shrewd
thrusts which enlivened good days and bad, merry evenings in
billets, wet and anxious nights in trenches. He left a gap that
could not be filled, a memory that could not be forgotten.

At the time of his death Valentine Fleming was still a
member of Parliament. Winston Churchill, who had been
on active duty with the Oxfordshire Hussars for a short
period during the war and who was familiar with Fleming's
career, wrote an obituary for *The Times*:

This news will cause sorrow in Oxfordshire and in the House
of Commons and wherever the member of the Henley Division
was well known. Valentine Fleming was one of those younger
Conservatives who easily and naturally combine loyalty to party
ties with a broad liberal outlook upon affairs and a total absence
of class prejudice. He was most earnest and sincere in his desire
to make things better for the great body of the people, and had
cleared his mind of all particularist tendencies. He was a man of
thoughtful and tolerant opinions, which were not the less strongly
or clearly held because they were not loudly or frequently asserted.
The violence of faction and the fierce tumults which swayed our
political life up to the very threshold of the Great War, caused
him a keen distress. He could not share the extravagant passions
with which the rival parties confronted each other. He felt acutely
that neither was wholly right in policy and that both were wrong
in mood. Although he could probably have held the Henley Division as long as he cared to fight it, he decided to withdraw from
public life rather than become involved in conflicts whose bitter-
ness seemed so far to exceed the practical issues at stake. Friends
were not wanting to encourage him to display the solid abilities
he possessed. It is possible we should have prevailed. He shared
the hopes to which so many of his generation respond of a better,

fairer, more efficient public life and Parliamentary system arising out of these trials. But events have pursued a different course.

As a Yeomanry officer he always took the greatest pains to fit himself for military duties. There was scarcely an instructional course open before the war to the Territorial Forces of which he had not availed himself, and on mobilization there were few more competent civilian soldiers of his rank. The Oxfordshire Hussars were the first or almost the first Yeomanry regiment to come under the fire of the enemy, and in the first battle of Ypres acquitted themselves with credit. He had been nearly three years in France, as squadron leader or second in command, and had been twice mentioned in dispatches, before the shell which ended his life found him. From the beginning his letters showed the deep emotions which the devastation and carnage of the struggle aroused in his breast. But the strength and buoyancy of his nature were proofs against the sombre realizations of his mind. He never for a moment flagged or wearied or lost his spirits. Alert, methodical, resolute, untiring he did his work, whether perilous or dull, without the slightest sign of strain or stress to the end. "We all of us," writes a brother officer, "were devoted to him. The loss to the regiment is indescribeable. He was, as you know, absolutely our best officer, utterly fearless, full of resource, and perfectly magnificent with his men." His passion in sport was deer stalking in his much loved native Scotland. He rode well and sometimes brilliantly to hounds, and was always a gay and excellent companion. He had everything in the world to make him happy; a delightful home life, active interesting expanding business occupations, contented disposition, a lovable and charming personality. He had more. He had that foundation of spontaneous and almost unconscious self-suppression in the discharge of what he conceived to be his duty without which happiness, however full, is precarious and imperfect. That these qualities are not singular in this generation does not lessen the loss of those in whom they shine. As the war lengthens and intensifies and the extending lists appear, it seems as if one watched at night a well-loved city whose lights, which burn so bright, which burn so true are extinguished in the distance in the darkness one by one.

Valentine Fleming was posthumously awarded the D.S.O. On November 10, 1917, *The Times* put the gross value of his estate at 265,596 pounds (well over one million dollars). By the terms of his will his salary as a member of Parliament during the war years was given in trust for the "relief of soldiers disabled in the war or their dependents residing in South Oxfordshire Division and who have served in the Oxfordshire Yeomanry or the Oxford and Buckingham Light Infantry." He was buried, with the other men who died in the attack on Gillemont Farm, in a little cemetery at St. Emilie.

So Valentine Fleming died in a chance raid on an isolated post. Aside from his considerable estate, he left to his son an ideal of service and duty which was not unusual, but which he had really lived by. He was not as spectacular a hero as that which his son later invented, but he was a very brave soldier who did what he thought he should do, always a difficult task.

He lived by the values of his time and place and tried to preserve these values. The son's values were not very different from those of the father, and in his own way Ian Fleming sought to preserve Edwardian ideals under far different conditions and in a far different world.

CHAPTER

2

Scoop

Unlike writers of the Norman Mailer school, who seem to believe that writing is merely another, and not entirely satisfactory, form of exhibitionism, Ian Fleming was always reticent about his personal affairs. He was not impressed by those who claim that the child is father to the man to such an extent that our later years are only a working out of our early sorrows. Because of these attitudes he never said much about his childhood, and since the members of his immediate family seem to share these beliefs, we have relatively little information on Fleming's early years.

We do know that the family was wealthy and the style of life grand but not ostentatious. Fleming, in an interview with Ken Purdy, called his childhood "overprivileged" and said that since all creative writers were by rule neurotic, he was also. He thought he was "rather melancholic, and probably slightly maniacal as well," but added that he had never been sufficiently interested in the subject to think very deeply about it.

Geoffrey Bocca in the *Saturday Evening Post* reports that Fleming was sent as a young boy to "an especially tough school which specialized in beating conformity into young children," but does not trouble with any further particulars.

Robert Harlach also speculated about Fleming's childhood. He wrote: "The English upper crust wants and needs affection as deeply as any other crust, but impulses towards this important emotional release are frequently stifled for them at about the age of eight when boys go away to boarding school. Affection by letter and postcard is as broken-backed as most other emotions by proxy. The boys grow up, professing to hate what they so need. Hence the undertones of sadism and masochism so frequent among British males. Hence, perhaps, those passages in the Bond books which have provoked such bitter attacks."

The first formative influence on Fleming about which we have any solid information is Eton, which Fleming attended, as did his father and his older brother Peter before him. Fleming seems to have had a somewhat ambivalent attitude toward Eton and the joys of public school. This is a rather common English trait, and somewhat parallels the feeling of many men for the army: that is to say, at the time the whole thing seems to be an unnecessary ordeal, but as it fades into memory you feel rather proud of yourself for having endured it and come to realize that it has strengthened your character in some inscrutable fashion and therefore should not be criticized, particularly by outsiders or those who did not make the grade.

Paul Gallico tells a story of wandering around Eton with Fleming after he had become a famous author and noticing that Fleming's normally florid face paled as he approached his old dormitory. He eventually found out that Fleming was reminiscing about a particularly painful episode. Fleming at Eton was a successful athlete but also somewhat high-spirited. He had accumulated a number of offenses and was caned by the headmaster just before the start of an important race. After this punishment Fleming ran and finished second, with blood streaming down the back of his legs. Gallico concluded: "Ian had one of the stiffest upper lips I have ever encountered upon any of my English friends. He was a courageous man."

William Plomer, who was at Eton at the same time as Fleming, recalls him as "an athlete of exceptional power." He was twice Victor Ludorum, or decathlon champion, the only boy ever to turn this trick, and before he was sixteen he had won every athletic event except the high jump. He attained his first taste of fame by these feats, for the news of his success traveled beyond Eton and he was featured in newsreels.

Plomer adds that Fleming was not merely a "small-brained muscle-boy." At Eton he possessed great intellectual curiosity, and eagerly sought out Plomer's first novel, which reviewers had called "volcanic." Plomer gives him credit for a "sharp flair, like that of a mine detector, for a new threat to dullness and complacency."

Fleming admitted there was a dark side to Eton, but seemed to think that the stiff upper lip could win through.

In a review he did for *The Sunday Times,* in 1962, of *The Fourth of June,* a novel by David Benedictus exposing Eton, he wrote: "Briefly the story is of Scarfe, a grammar school boy, bent and finally broken by the snobbery, sadism and sexuality (hetero-, homo-, and auto-) which in the Benedictian view, are the devils in the machine of an Eton education . . .

"Knowing nothing of the strains and stresses suffered by the modern Scarfes beneath the weight of Eton and its customs, it is difficult for an older Etonian not to argue that in his day the psychologically halt and lame boys also went to the wall, and he might complain, I think legitimately, that the author has outstripped the bounds of truth in laying Scarfe's downfall to the three S's mentioned above . . ."

Fleming did not deny that these three S's (to which many critics assign a prominent place in his fiction) existed at Eton. He merely says that they are not, in the last analysis, that important. In another article he was more explicit about these matters. He says he was "bullied at school and lost my virginity like so many of us used to do in the old days."

This homosexuality in English public schools is accepted as more or less a matter of course and nothing much to write home about. It is a phase through which some boys pass and to which other boys are subjected, and nothing more. Another current English author, Simon Raven, mentions being expelled from another school for homosexual practices, but he neither exalts them lyrically, after the manner of recent French or American writers, nor takes an overly dim view of his own guilt. It was just something he did at the time.

After Eton, Fleming went on to Sandhurst, the English

equivalent of West Point, and not to Oxford, where his brother Peter had a brilliant career as a student at Christ Church College; Peter was president of the Oxford University Dramatic Society and an editor of *Isis,* the student literary magazine, and he took a first in English.

At Sandhurst, Ian received a commission in a cavalry regiment but turned it down because "they were mechanizing the Army, and a lot of us decided we didn't want to be garage hands running those bloody tanks." This is an interesting comment, because it echoes that theme of the vulgarity of so much of modern life which repeats itself in the Bond novels. War, of course, is not primarily an aesthetic activity, and despite the lack of "polo" and "pigsticking," which Fleming apparently identified with the great days of the cavalry regiments, it is a fact that the British Army did not mechanize sufficiently between the two wars (partially because of this old-cavalry-hands attitude which Fleming shared), and as a result was almost blitzkrieged out of existence in the early days of World War II.

(It would be simple-minded to suggest that Ian Fleming, as a Sandhurst graduate who did not ever enter the Army, had anything whatsoever to do with this. I am merely noting that he shared a fondness for the past Edwardian glory which is common in present-day England, and that this has something to do with both the strengths and the deficiencies of his later work.)

The decision to drop out of the army, Fleming said, infuriated his mother, who insisted that he do something, "something respectable," and compared him unfavorably with his older brothers, who were all doing "splendidly." Ian opted for the Foreign Service and went abroad to study languages at the University of Geneva and the University of Munich. He learned to speak and write fluent French and German and picked up a smattering of Russian. He later felt that this was the most important part of his education and "a tremendous extension of one's life generally," while all the other things he had learned at Eton and Sandhurst were completely forgotten.

After two years in Germany and Switzerland, Ian came home and took the Foreign Service examination. He finished seventh, and there were only five openings, so the Foreign Service was out and he was once again without a career. The year was 1931 and the depression was well under way. Fleming was 23, and aside from studying at a number of different schools he had done nothing but some book collecting. He looked around for a job that would make some use of his talents and education, and eventually found it.

He got it through a friend of his mother's, Sir Roderick Jones, who was then chairman of Reuters. Fleming wrote Sir Roderick a letter, enclosing a letter of recommendation from a mutual acquaintance. Ian's letter is as follows:

Dear Sir Roderick,

I don't expect you will remember me, although we did once meet at a party here. I hope you won't think me presumptuous taking advantage of your friendship with my mother in order to write to you personally. My object in doing so is, briefly, as follows.

I have just taken the Foreign Office exam and passed adequately, but not brilliantly. In the normal course of events I should try again, but I have decided not to, as I am really longing to start regular work as soon as possible.

My education has been "international" above all else—Eton-

Munich University-Geneva University—"Hautes Etudes Internationales" at Geneva and various minor institutions such as the "Foyer des Etudes Slaves" at Paris etc. My languages are essentially practical, i.e. conversational, yet in the F.O. exam I got 70% for both French and German and 56% for Russian. I have a good knowledge of Psychology and a Swiss "certificate" in Anthropology. I worked for the Austrian government in the Secretariat of the League of Nations (Section for Intellectual Cooperation) and have translated one book and several articles from the German.

I have mentioned these facts in order to give you a vague idea of my capabilities and interests, and in the hope that you might consider the possibility of my being of use to Reuters. I have been given an idea of the work at Reuters, and I can only say that there is no profession I should prefer or to which I should devote myself with so much enthusiasm.

These are vain words and I should very much like to come and see you, if you think there is any chance of my getting into Reuters. Could you spare me a moment any day early next week?

These are hard times and I expect you are chary of engaging any new staff. I shall be all the more grateful should you decide to take me on.

Yours sincerely,
Ian Fleming

The letter of recommendation is of some interest, for it gives a fairly good idea of the circles Ian Fleming and his family moved in and the kind of interest he could enlist when looking for a job. It reads:

Dear Sir:

With reference to the enclosed I beg to say that I have known Mr. Ian Fleming all his life. His parents & grandparents have been my intimate friends for many years.

His grandfather is one of the most able, best known & highly respected men of business in the City of London & his father,

M.-P. for South Oxfordshire, was a man of outstanding qualities.

He has therefore been brought up in surroundings where he has had the advantage of being associated with culture, practical business experience & knowledge of the world. He is personally a young man of great intelligence, energy & promise, thoroughly well educated.

He has been employed at the League of Nations Council; & I have heard the most satisfactory accounts of the impression made by him there. He has an excellent brain, & very good manners. He is quick & extremely intelligent. I can highly recommend him in every respect.

He should have a distinct (sic) career before him.

Yours faithfully,
Robert White

With this recommendation of his family and general breeding, and given the fact that in England it is very important to know the right people, it might be assumed that Fleming was certain of getting a position with Reuters. However, the English newspaper world is a fairly rough-and-tumble place and one of the few places where the old boys' network is not completely effective. Editors were actually more interested in having men who got the story first than in those who spoke with the correct accent. Fleming was also correct in assuming that few people were going out of their way to hire inexperienced personnel at that time.

In spite of these considerations, Fleming had come at the right moment. Sir Roderick Jones was trying to improve Reuters' position with regard to the American competition, and he had the notion that a few public school boys such as Fleming might improve the tone of Reuters' dispatches. Fleming got the job and his mother wrote to Sir Roderick, thanking him. She said:

My dear Sir Roderick,

   I *am* so glad to hear that you are giving Ian a trial. I am disappointed in a way that he is not having another try for the F.O. exam, as we never expected him to get in this year. However I am delighted that he passed the exam & if you find him useful it may be all for the best! He loved his first day with you & I do hope you will like him. He has great character & is supposed to be very intelligent, though I ought not to say so! I am just back & hope to see you & Enid soon—

Yours v. sincerely,

   Working for Reuters, Fleming came under the supervision of Mr. Bernard Rickatson-Hatt, a monocled former Guards officer. Rickatson-Hatt's first impression of Fleming was by and large favorable. He sent an interoffice memo to Sir Roderick, dated October 21, 1931, which stated:

Young FLEMING started working in the Editorial Department last Monday (October 19th).
   So far, he has made an excellent impression. You will appreciate that it is rather early to say anything definite, but I believe he may be worth a trial.
   His languages are sound. His appearance is good, and his manners are agreeable.
   He suffers, perhaps, from a slight Foreign Office "bump," but I think you can depend on us to put some pep into him before many days have gone by.

   Fleming survived his month's trial period and showed himself to be a diligent, persevering reporter. Recalling this period after his later success, he said that news agency work in the early thirties was "like a gigantic football match" and proved "highly enjoyable." He told Ken Purdy: "In those days the paper came first, the story came first, you were out to beat hell out of the opposition, and the pay and the hours of work meant nothing."

This kind of spirit soon earned him the plaudits of Rickatson-Hatt, who sent him a note of commendation on April 19, 1932, which read:

We have received the following letter from Mr. O. R. Hobson, the Editor-in-Chief of the FINANCIAL NEWS:

"I understand from our Night Staff that Mr. Fleming of your office was extremely helpful Friday night in getting for us back figures on German and French foreign trade, and that he went to much trouble to assist us.

"I should be very glad if you would be kind enough to express to him our appreciation of his efforts."

This is excellent work on your part and shows the right spirit. Anything that you can ever do to oblige papers in this way is well worth the trouble.

Fleming also won over his superiors at Reuters by his attention to detail and his willingness to take on niggling little assignments. For example, he drew up a new editorial order on the obituary section of the editorial index, and there is again a memo from Rickatson-Hatt relating to this which reads: "This is good work on his part. He is thorough and scholarly and has made a good job of this. It was something that badly wanted doing."

After a year of hard work and beating the opposition, Fleming had convinced himself that he was well on the way to becoming a good newspaperman and he wrote to Sir Roderick Jones, asking him to double his salary. This was not as outrageous a request as it might appear to be on the surface since, for the first year at Reuters, Fleming had received the very nominal salary of 150 pounds (about 850 dollars at that time), and even keeping in mind that the cost of living in 1931 was considerably lower than it is at present, this was hardly enough to keep a fashionable young man with expensive tastes.

He told Sir Roderick he was delighted with his work and "enthusiastic . . . about the whole organization," but that "the day is past when a career is merely a hobby." He added that he had been for twenty-four years "from the financial point of view at least . . . a dead loss to my family," and said that he considered it his duty to start earning a living.

Then Fleming went on to say that he regarded his first year as training and realized that the firm had undertaken to train him as an investment. He wrote: "You took a risk, and I am naturally anxious to know whether you consider that risk justified."

He wanted to know whether the management thought that he had a future with Reuters, because he had an offer from the banking firm of Robert Fleming & Co. Fleming wanted to stay with Reuters and considered the banking situation not at all in accordance with his preferences or ambition. "But," he wrote, "I know you will appreciate the fact that I owe to my family and to myself to assure my future as far as possible."

The upshot of all this was that he would leave unless Reuters reassured him about being wanted to the tune of another 150 pounds a year, for "I do feel that I am either worth £300 a year to the firm or else, in my opinion, nothing at all."

Fleming got his raise, in two stages, and Sir Roderick wrote a note to the chief accountant saying that "a definite exception is being made for him because of the special circumstances of his case," the special circumstances being that he could very easily get another job paying more money and that Reuters, after employing him for a year, didn't want to lose him.

About this same period there is another memorandum from Rickatson-Hatt dated October 19, 1932, evidently replying to an inquiry as to the quality of Fleming's work. It may well have had some bearing on the raise he asked for and received. The memo reads in part:

> This is the work that Fleming is now doing.
> This particular "obit" is based on one of the several hundred A.P. biographies which they gave me when I was in New York and which I brought back with me last year.
> Fleming is doing these extremely well.
> He is accurate, painstaking, and methodical. He also has a good business instinct—doubtless a family trait.

The sample obit which Rickatson-Hatt included with his memo is about the "Death of the Marquis de Castellane. 'Boni', the Prince of Extravagance. Famous Marriage and Divorce. Most Conspicuous Figure in Paris Society."

There is little point in quoting this extensively. The basic work was done by the AP and Fleming was merely rewriting these advance obits, which Rickatson-Hatt hoped that the "provincials, at least," would use, for the English market. The Marquis de Castellane has long since been totally forgotten, and Fleming was hardly in a position to put any personal touches into this kind of work.

(However, in the rewrite he did make one rather odd grammatical blunder. Toward the end of the obit the following sentence appears: "Since the war his place in Paris society had been more effaced." The mistake was duly noted by whoever received the obit along with Rickatson-Hatt's memo, for the offending phrase is circled and there are two exclamation marks in the margin. The error is even odder when we remember that Ian Fleming always aspired to "unexceptionable" grammar and always attained it. There is, however, probably no very deep-seated explanation of this solitary miscue, other than that rewrite men often turn out large quantities of work and get rather punchy in the process.)

So Ian Fleming worked for well over a year at Reuters, learning his trade by rewriting advance obits and all the other unexciting jobs which young men at a news agency are expected to take on. He had proved himself as a capable man, one that the agency thought enough of to give what was evidently an unusually high raise after a year's work.

He was well thought of by his contemporaries and his elders. Alaric Jacob, who started with him on Fleet Street, recalled: "Such good judges as Harold Nicolson and Robert Vansittart predicted great things for Ian Fleming. With his strong facial resemblance to Vansittart, Ian was then an *ambassador manque.* . . . He was not, at the start, a brilliant journalist: others of our circle . . . progressed much faster than he, but behind Ian's languid good looks, the canny Scots way he had of deploying his talents and his delightful capacity for friendship many people detected a glittering potential."

Others at the time had this same impression of a man

who would someday do great things, but no one seemed
quite sure of what they would be. William Plomer recalled
in *Encounter* meeting him at a garden party given by his
mother: "He was youthfully handsome himself, wearing a
well-cut dark blue suit and with very good manners, easy,
cheerful and welcoming. . . . He seemed to me to have good
luck on his side—youth, health, strength, money, general
eligibility, a social status taken for granted, work that interested him, and a consciousness of his powers. At that first
encounter he struck me as no mere conventional young
English man-of-the-world of his generation; he showed more
character, a much quicker brain, and a promise of something dashing or daring. Like a mettlesome young horse, he
seemed to show the whites of his eyes and to smell battle
from afar."

In the spring of 1933 this promising young man received
his first important newspaper assignment and at the same
time came into contact with the world of darkness, secrecy,
strange lies and stranger truth which he was later to make
peculiarly his own.

On March 13, 1933, *The Times* of London reported:
"BRITISH SUBJECTS ARRESTED, ACTION BY OGPU
IN MOSCOW." The brief story told how Alan Monkhouse,
W. H. Thornton, John Cushny, and W. H. Macdonald, all
of whom were employed by the Metro-Vickers Company
of Manchester, had been arrested by the secret police along
with a Latvian and four Russians who worked for the company. Monkhouse had been taken by some half-dozen OGPU
men, who had surrounded his house while he was eating
dinner, and the company's offices had been raided and its
records seized. Later, two other British subjects, A. W.

Gregory and C. de Nordwall, were arrested on the same charge.

At first, no one in England seemed to have any idea what this was all about. The arrested men were engineers working on various construction projects in Russia. Mr. George Bailey, the general manager of Metro-Vickers, told *The Times*:

"The news has come as a big surprise to the company. We have considerable commercial interests in Russia, where we are engaged in construction work, and the four men whose arrests are reported are four of our senior men in the country. They were engaged in an advisory capacity, and I am quite confident that neither they nor any member of the company in Russia have done anything that would be contrary to Russian policy. We are sure that some mistake has been made and we are taking every measure we can to safeguard the interests both of the men and of the company."

The early reports of this affair in the English papers seem somewhat naive. They express a mixture of shock and incredulity. Various statements were produced speculating about the nature of the crimes the four engineers had committed and whether or not they were guilty of these acts. It only gradually occurred to the newsmen that the entire question of an actual offense and of guilt or innocence might be totally irrelevant to those who had ordered the arrests. As it turned out, these arrests were a staged affair which enabled the government to find scapegoats for economic difficulties with which the four men had nothing to do. The possibility of such a conception of criminal justice only slowly occurred to anyone in England.

It was in these first days of speculation as to the charges that were to be preferred against the Metro-Vickers men that Ian Fleming first entered the case. He wrote a story, which was released with a Riga dateline, saying that the men would be charged with espionage in connection with the construction of Dnieprostroy Dam. Specifically, Fleming's article speculated that the men were to be accused of corroding the blades of the turbines of the dam "with malicious intent." According to this idea, the blades of the turbines had corroded, and "since the blades were made of rustless steel of the very finest quality, sand or acid must have been poured into the turbines in order to bring about the alleged corrosion which could not otherwise have occurred."

Since this was the first specific information on the nature of the accusation against the Metro-Vickers engineers, the story created an overnight sensation in England and for a time got Fleming in a little hot water. The story was carried by the BBC, who did not contact Metro-Vickers before carrying it. Metro-Vickers was extremely indignant about the story, particularly since, as I have said, it was then in the minds of the English public that the Russian government was incapable of making up out of whole cloth whatever accusations it needed in order to cover up administrative blunders.

Metro-Vickers issued several denials, one of which said: ". . . the idea of damaging these heavy turbines by pouring in sand or acid is manifestly absurd.

"Each blade used in these machines weighs about five tons, and millions of gallons of water pass through the turbines daily, which would prevent any acid or sand remaining in them. The statement that the charge against the men is of such a nature, therefore, is fantastic."

Metro-Vickers went on to state that it had furnished very little material for the dam in question and ended by once again expressing a pious view: "The company is still confident that the whole affair is a terrible mistake and that all the employees there under arrest ought to be released at once."

Fleming had gotten his story from a friend of his who was employed by Metro-Vickers. When the company issued its categorical denial of the story and when the *News-Chronicle,* a paper Rickatson-Hatt characterized as "very Russophile," ridiculed the story, the Reuters staff naturally wanted to know further details of how it had come in. Fleming wrote a memorandum for Rickatson-Hatt describing how he had obtained this break. It read, in part, as follows:

1. The story originated from a friendly conversation with Mr. Gerald Coke, of Industrial Steels Ltd in the Vickers Combine, who told me the latest facts as ascertained by Mr. Anthony Vickers. At the same time, he emphasized that the charges were fantastic, as was expected, but not mechanically impossible. Perhaps the "fantastic" angle was not sufficiently emphasized in my story.

On reading our story and the denials in Monday's papers Mr. Anthony Vickers told Mr. Coke that there was no ground for the denials, as our facts were substantially correct and the alleged corrosion was by no means the impossible phenomenon [sic] alleged in their denial by Metro-Vickers. . . .

According to Fleming, Vickers also told Mr. Coke that there were certain technical errors in Fleming's story but that these were "quibbles" and that "the backbone of our story, that the arrests were connected with Dnieprostroi dam, was the latest news he himself had obtained." Fleming's memorandum concluded by saying that Vickers would not, however, permit himself to be quoted as contradicting the statements made at Metro-Vickers and that "he would object most strongly to use being made of his name following friendly conversation."

Rickatson-Hatt's memorandum exonerated Fleming: "I am convinced that Fleming acted in good faith. I don't think either that he was victimized by Vickers. As you know, he is a most intelligent fellow and also very careful and conscientious in his work. On the other hand, he should have made it clear that his story was obtained from a personal friend and not necessarily authorised for publication."

This memo goes into great detail about how the story was checked with the Foreign Office before it was put out and then about the reasons it was issued with a Riga dateline. Then Fleming's editor makes a rather shrewd guess. "It is very curious," Rickatson-Hatt writes, "that we have heard nothing from Tass. As a rule, the moment we issue anything here from Riga, it is sent back to Moscow and denied almost as a matter of routine. It is very significant that Tass has sent nothing on this occasion. This rather lends colour to the supposition that the Soviet authorities may actually be bringing these very charges against the British engineers, however fantastic and ridiculous the accusations may appear."

The memorandum concludes: "In my opinion, the whole affair was a storm in a teacup, and I don't think we shall hear very much more, if anything, about it."

At this distance it is impossible to sort out the story fully. Charges of wrecking at the Dnieprostroy Dam were not filed against the Metro-Vickers people, but similar charges of wrecking on other projects were. The mistake everyone, including Fleming, was making was in assuming that the people such as Vyshinsky, who prosecuted the Metro-Vickers case, would be much bothered if their accusations were demonstrated to be fantastic.

The idea of a fair trial is really very deeply ingrained in English and American minds. Even a frame-up, in a detective story (or in fact), is based on false evidence that fits together to form a convincing picture of guilt. The Russians, when preparing their political trials, simply didn't trouble themselves about this kind of thing. Their ideas of justice were much grander and did not rest on picayune details of fact. If a defendant had not actually done what he was accused of, if in fact no one could possibly have done what the charge stated, that did not matter, for the defendant represented a social class or process that was condemned by history. Thus a defendant in the purge trials of later years "confessed" to putting ground glass in tons of food, a patently ridiculous notion; but that did not matter, for the defendant, even if he didn't know it, was an enemy of the state and the party and must be swept into oblivion by the true representatives of the historical process.

Shortly before the Metro-Vickers trial opened, *The Times* published an article which clarified this subject for the English public. They pointed out that N. V. Krylenko, then Commissar of Justice, had written: "In the specific nature of their functions there is no difference of character between the Soviet Court of Justice and the Cheka. . . . Every Judge must keep himself well informed on questions of State policy and remember that his judicial decisions in particular cases are intended to promote just the prevailing policy of the ruling class and nothing else."

The Times also mentioned that Vyshinsky had written that the idea of "general justice" was a pretense, and quoted this passage from a textbook used by law students at Moscow University:

"Soviet law has never recognized and does not recognize the principle that all persons are equal in the eyes of the law. All decrees of the Soviet Government and all Soviet laws have from the beginning taken great care to insist on a strict class-line. It would be very naive to afford equality of justice to the toiler and the class-enemy. This would be contrary to the policy of the Soviet Government."

All this, however, only gradually became apparent to the Western world. The trials which later condemned Bukharin, Trotsky and other leading Communists were defended by intellectually respectable people who simply could not see what was fairly obvious, that millions of innocent people were being condemned by the champions of socialism in one country. At the time the Metro-Vickers engineers were arrested, these purges were only about to begin and the Soviet concept of justice was not known to many in the West. This trial, however, was closely observed, particularly in England, and it must have opened some eyes. Among the people with the best chance to observe these strange proceedings was Ian Fleming.

Fleming knew Russian and he had broken a story on the Metro-Vickers case that had received a lot of play. It may not have been thought wise to cover the Metro-Vickers trial with Reuters' regular Moscow correspondent, as it was apparent by the time the trial opened that the charges were not going to be very convincing and that the English press would have to deal fairly harshly with the case. It is often difficult for a regular correspondent to deal critically with people he depends on as his sources of news. In any event, a memo from Rickatson-Hatt dated April 5, 1933, states that he had briefed Fleming before he departed for Moscow to cover the Metro-Vickers trial.

Even before the trial opened, certain facts had become apparent. The British press had started to notice that the Russians were having difficulties with their plans for rapid industrialization and that these difficulties were being blamed on counterrevolutionary "wreckers." It is inevitable in any country where modern industrial facilities are placed in the hands of inexperienced managers and workers that some of this machinery will break down because it is mishandled and that grandiose notions of what can be accomplished by industrialization will prove to be deceptive. (This same process currently is taking place in many parts of Africa and Asia.) In a centralized, bureaucratized economy, this process probably is accentuated because of massive errors in judgment made by the centralized managers.

However, in a totalitarian state it is simply impossible for the state to admit that plans which it has propagandized are failing because the men in charge have overestimated the human potential of the workers and managers. (It is possible for lower-ranking bureaucrats to be guilty of ordinary human stupidity and mismanagement, but it is inconceivable that a whole plan could have been a mistake.) Nevertheless, there comes a time when the advertised benefits of the plan have not appeared and it is obvious that something has gone wrong. At this point, counterrevolu-

tionaries are discovered and evidence of widespread espionage is produced; this is what happened in Russia at the
time of the Metro-Vickers trial.

Fleming in his coverage of the trial had this whole process
demonstrated for him in detail. While he was still in England, the Commissar for Heavy Industry announced that
Russia was being "swindled" on a great scale by foreign
firms, and that defective machinery was "largely responsible
for the inferior quality of Soviet industrial output." This
plot was linked in the press to "opposition" leaders and a
nationalist note was sounded by warning that the Soviet
government would not brook foreign interference and that
all "discovered wreckers" would be tried regardless of their
nationality.

The Soviets particularly objected to the adverse comments of the English press (which they labeled "diehard")
and ranted: "Why could not the diehards contain themselves
when the OGPU unmasked the plot and quietly await the
results of the investigation and the official pronouncement
of the Soviet court? These gentlemen were afraid of publicity and therefore endeavoured to segregate the British
citizens from the band of Russian malefactors and secure
them impunity for crimes committed and discovered, of
which the Soviet authorities obtained proofs and the prisoners' own confessions. Obviously, the diehards overestimated their powers, forgetting that the USSR is an independent country and that all within the Soviet boundaries
must submit to Soviet laws irrespective of their nationality."

Shortly after Fleming arrived in Moscow, the nature of
Soviet justice and the confessions the prisoners had signed
were made manifest by a British White Paper on the sub-

ject. According to this report, a representative of the Embassy had interviewed Mr. Thornton on April 4th and had reported:

Mr. Thornton is worn out, and it was not easy to get a connected story from him. He has been under interrogation from the day of his arrest until this morning, on one occasion for about 21 hours without a break. He found suspense of waiting for the next summons and perpetual tramping up and down stairs in a heavy coat most exhausting. He was never directly threatened or offered a straight bargain for a "confession," but there was a strong undercurrent of menacing hints during his examination and occasional suggestions of lucrative employment in return for satisfactory answers. He was confronted with Mr. Cushny and Mr. Macdonald and many Russians, including Mme. Kutsova (the company's secretary), sometimes unexpectedly. Russians made most fantastic accusations against him, and were either in a state of terror or obviously in league with GPU. He was many times deliberately misled, e.g.—

1. He was told that all the company's British employees in Russia had been arrested.

2. He was given daily bulletins of Mr. Monkhouse's health to make him think Mr. Monkhouse was still in prison.

3. Examiners read to him what purported to be Mr. Monkhouse's statements in his deposition regarding two instances of failure of plant supplied by company some years ago ... to which Mr. Monkhouse had, in fact, made no reference whatever in his deposition.

When the indictment was released, it accused six Metro-Vickers engineers of the following activities (according to *The Times* summary):

1. Damaging plant in order to undermine Soviet industry and weaken the Soviet State.

2. Collecting and utilizing to damage of State secret information of military and State importance.

3. Bribing of employees of State electricity stations in connection with execution by them of counterrevolutionary wrecking activities.

It is interesting to note that "wrecking" activities figured prominently in the indictments against all of the English engineers, as Fleming's story had been the first to state. The charges were neither more nor less fantastic than his story had originally detailed, although the specific dam which Fleming had mentioned was not an important part of the prosecution's case.

To sustain these allegations, the prosecution relied on the corroborating testimony of a number of Soviet citizens who either were employed by Metro-Vickers or had worked with them on certain projects. Their abject confessions were exactly in the style which was later made familiar to the world in the purge trials, and the prosecutor, Vyshinsky, operated in his usual fashion.

The Russians had attempted to break down all of the Metro-Vickers engineers, and had gotten incriminating statements from most of them. In the course of their examination, they had evidently detected weaknesses in Mr. Macdonald and concentrated most of their attention on him; as a result, he made a confession to many amazing deeds. The indictment stated:

Gusev's [a Russian engineer] chief activity was, however, organization of breakdowns at Zlatoust power station, which he says began at Macdonald's instigation about the middle of 1930 with object of lowering production of shells and high quality steel.

Macdonald confirms this ("I told Gusev that as a means of fighting against Soviet regime creation of breakdowns in production should be utilized at most important point") . . . Gusev gives details of various wrecking acts carried out on Macdonald's instructions, disabling of motors and coal conveyors, freezing boilers.

At confrontations with Gusev, Macdonald states that he gave Gusev instructions to disable coal conveyors and certain boilers. He further states: "I had as my object direct disorganization of electricity supply of Zlatoust works which would decrease work of military production.

"I chose as a means the reduction of output of power station by half. In this event slightest breakdown would have caused complete paralysis of works."

The indictment details various breakdowns at six separate power plants, all due to the criminal machinations of the Metro-Vickers engineers, and these allegations were sustained by OGPU confessions extorted from Russian citizens and Macdonald.

The usual smooth course of Soviet justice was interrupted many times by the intractable nature of five of the six English defendants. (Macdonald, after making his confession, pleaded guilty.) Several of them had made certain admissions during the interrogations which they denied at the trial. On the first day of the trial, the Russian engineer Gusev told about his various wrecking activities and Macdonald was called upon to admit that the accusations were true. But Thornton had recovered somewhat from the OGPU and changed his story. Fleming's account of this incident follows:

Mr. Thornton was called, and admitted meeting Gusev and Mr. Macdonald in a station buffet in the Ural Mountains. He said that he was aware Gusev gave information to Mr. Macdonald concerning his firm's business, but he was not aware that there was any question of espionage—"I do not know what you mean by espionage."

Judge Ulrich interposed, remarking: "It is a bad word." He then read to Mr. Thornton certain passages from his alleged depositions contained in the indictment, where he admitted cognizance of espionage activities.

Vyshinsky asked, "Is that true?" Mr. Thornton paused, and then in a loud, clear voice said "No." "Then why did you admit it on March 15?"—"I was nervous."

"Did they apply third degree methods? Did you suffer?"— "No," answered Mr. Thornton.

Gusev, after four hours in the witness box, was very nervous. He spoke in a trembling voice, his face twitching with emotion. He admitted all the accusations against him, and said that if his life was spared he could reform and become a good Soviet citizen.

The second day of the trial was its climax from the dramatic point of view. Mr. Macdonald had been the only one of the English engineers to plead guilty; he had made an extensive confession implicating his colleagues. During the course of the day's proceedings he retracted his confession, and then after an intermission called by the judges, retracted his retraction.

Macdonald changed his plea in the morning of the second day of the trial to not guilty. *The Times* reported that "Macdonald ignored his own defending counsel . . . and informed the Court that his depositions against himself, against Mr. Thornton, and against others were a tissue of lies, signed 'under the pressure of circumstances' on the premises of the OGPU."

The prosecutor urged him to reconsider and Macdonald

replied: "I certainly pleaded guilty, but I am not really guilty. I gave no orders to organize sabotage, and I emphatically deny my former statement. I was forced by circumstances. . . . I thought it would be better for me to sign the protocol in which my supposed crimes were set out. But I am not really guilty of these crimes. I declare this emphatically. Moreover, I did not see the translation and I do not know that the Russian text is exact. . . . When the examining magistrate read to me in prison the affidavit of Thornton confessing to espionage, I felt hopeless and that it was of no use to deny it. I felt apathetic."

After Macdonald had dropped his bombshell (for his was the only non-Russian testimony Vyshinsky could count on), Mr. Thornton, according to *The Times,* "said he had made false admissions in prison because he had 'lost his courage!' Asked when he had regained it, he said, 'At 6 P.M. on April 4' (i.e. when released on bail)."

The Times' Moscow correspondent commented, "The Prosecutor and Judges did not conceal their annoyance at this 'unwarranted interference' with their plan, as the entire case now rests on the confessions of the Russian prisoners, which lack weight, as everyone can imagine how they were obtained."

The court then adjourned and after Macdonald had left the court with his OGPU guard, he returned and "there was a change in his behaviour which was remarked by all observers. He was again questioned as to whether he admitted espionage, and replied in low tones in the affirmative. He also stated that the collective information involved was suggested by Mr. Thornton, and that he presumed other

Metro-Vickers engineers were implicated. He also admitted
giving instructions for machine wrecking. . . .

"Before the Court adjourned Mr. Macdonald was giving
his evidence almost in a state of collapse, and answered in
reply to the Prosecutor that he had made a certain petition
jointly to the Ogpu and the Prosecutor when in prison."

Thornton, on the other hand, persisted in denying everything, including the admissions he had made while in the
hands of the OGPU, in spite of the persistent badgering of
Vyshinsky. Thornton never accused the OGPU of "third
degree methods," which Vyshinsky continually asked him
about, but said he was "agitated" while in the hands of the
OGPU. In fact, it was unlikely that the Russians physically
mistreated their prisoners; this could be embarrassing in the
case of foreigners, who did not always stick to their confessions, and was, in any event, unnecessary. The OGPU
had already learned that by keeping certain men awake for
long periods of time and continually confronting them with
accusations of fellow prisoners, they could produce the
desired results.

During the next day's testimony the Dnieprostroy Dam
project was mentioned, which must have been gratifying to
Fleming. A Russian named Siebert, after saying that he
had been paid to sabotage by Thornton, then claimed that
Gregory (a very unsatisfactory defendant from Vyshinsky's
point of view, since he wouldn't admit anything) had
"started counter-Soviet propaganda" as soon as he had come
to Dnieprostroy. Gregory denied this, saying that he couldn't
speak Russian, that he had more than enough work to do,
and that he wasn't interested in politics.

At the start of the last day's testimony, Mr. Monkhouse grabbed the microphones and loudly declared that the whole trial was a "frame-up." *The Times* reported: "Almost at the opening of the Court Mr. Monkhouse assumed that he had permission to speak and immediately began:—'I declare the whole trial is a frame-up constructed on entirely false confessions by terrorized Russians.' The Judges interrupted him several times, but Monkhouse adroitly moved closer to the microphone (which is not connected with the broad-casting station, but is a convenience within the hall) and continued amid a certain hubbub. His exact words were difficult to gather, but their gist was clear. Mr. Monkhouse proclaimed the whole proceedings a farce, because he knew better than anyone the value of confessions obtained within the Ogpu's prison. He himself had been subjected to inter-rogation uninterruptedly for 18 hours, and evidence obtained in such conditions was valueless."

Monkhouse was finally shut up and Vyshinsky later pro-duced OGPU records to show that Monkhouse had only been interrogated for some 12 to 13 hours after he was first arrested, but for the rest of the day the unruly defendants persisted in denying the charges against them and Mr. Cushny stated that the Russians who were giving testimony against him were "perjuring themselves."

The well-ordered spectacle which Vyshinsky and his col-leagues had planned turned out rather badly. All of the defendants (except Macdonald) insisted that the Russians giving testimony against them were mistaken, and several insisted that these Russians had been terrorized by the OGPU. Macdonald, the only satisfactorily repentant Eng-lishman, was in some respects Vyshinsky's worst exhibit, for the spectacle of him retracting his confession and then, after a session with the OGPU, saying that he had been right in the first place was not an edifying one. Several of the engineers had made the point that the "wrecking" they were accused of was more likely due to a combination of ordinary mechanical breakdowns and inexperienced Russian personnel, and neither the witnesses nor the prosecution seemed to be particularly well informed about these matters.

In spite of this, Vyshinsky's summation for the prosecution was delivered in precisely that vicious style for which he later became notorious throughout the world. A few particulars from Fleming's Reuters' dispatch are worth quoting. Pointing his finger at the defendants, Vyshinsky proclaimed: "You are the last remnants of the technical intelligentzia. Against you are honest Soviet workers. The Soviet is too strong to fear you. As for Monkhouse and Thornton, their crimes are too disgusting, and I can find no words for them. They are worse than the Russian prisoners."

Vyshinsky's speech was somewhat defensive, for the Russians had been stung by reports of the trial which criticized Soviet justice. He said, "We will not allow anyone to interfere with our internal affairs, and this must be remembered. Capitalists do not like our Court because it is a class Court. . . . Karl Marx says of English Courts that there is one for justice for the poor and one for the rich, and in India the same third degree methods are used as in the case of Lieutenant Baillie-Stewart. We have the only true justice in the world."

Later the representative of the only true justice in the world pointed at Mr. Thornton and said, "You will be no use in Russia or England. Perhaps, you will be used as manure for our Socialist fields somewhere."

Vyshinsky was hard-pressed at times for evidence to prove his indictment and several times brought up rather trivial information as proof of serious crimes. For example, he said in summation: "Thornton said he only knew that guns and aeroplanes made a noise. Then why did you need Macdonald? Why did you need to bribe? Nonsense—child's talk!

"Thornton gave eau de cologne, a pair of trousers, and other things to a certain person. These, Mr. Thornton, were bribes and methods of getting information."

Vyshinsky concluded in what was, for him, a charitable mood. He said, "I say they are all guilty under Article 58, carrying sentences up to shooting, but it is necessary to consider their failure as a mitigating circumstance. . . .

"In your verdict you must remember that the Soviet Government does not seek the blood of vengeance, but the defence of the Socialist revolution. You must not forget in your verdict that our country is already strong enough to resist counter-revolution. We are not revengeful and cruel, but, if you find it necessary to invoke the highest measure of social defence, your hands must not tremble. That measure is contained in Article 58, which I invoke."

The defense speeches were, of course, far more moderate in tone. *The Times* characterized them as "non-committal" and noted that only one of the defense lawyers asked for an acquittal, although all the defendants (again except Macdonald) pleaded not guilty. The English defendants all made short speeches in their own behalf in which they categorically denied the evidence against them. Mr. Monkhouse did not repeat his charge of a "frame-up" but did make one interesting point about the wrecking charge that had been made against them all. He noted that the Soviet government then owed his company 1,500,000 pounds, and continued: "It would be cutting our own throats to do wrecking, which would destroy or lessen the Soviet capacity to pay. I have been very proud of the fact that during the last eight years I have taken an enormous part in the development of electrification in this country. As the present head of Metro-Vickers in Russia I have done everything to help in that work, and I have taken a natural pride in being associated with it. It is incomprehensible how it could be brought against me that I was associated with wrecking. We engineers look on our work as our own children. I never met a mother who would plunge a dagger in her own child's heart."

But the verdict was in before the trial started. Even before it was announced, the Russian press was celebrating a famous victory over the capitalists. *The Times* reported: "Most of the Soviet newspapers published poems or 'hymns of victory' specially written for the occasion, telling in rhymed and unrhymed verse how the proletarians overcame wreckers; recording in advance the Court's judgment of guilty; and stating that sharp justice was done to the wreckers.

"Today, which is a Soviet holiday, the prisoners and trial served as the subject of entertainments, in which there were recitations and songs defying them and all capitalists. Mr. Thornton had an entire doggerel poem to himself. The teachers first recited it to gatherings of school children, and then the children sang it to popular tunes."

Moscow, May 1, 1933. As a correspondent for Reuters Ian Fleming scored impressive scoops at the notorious Soviet trial of British and Russian employees of England's Metro-Vickers Company. Here the defendants await their sentence on trumped up charges of espionage and sabotage. *United Press International Photo.*

Photograph on the previous page from *London Daily Express.*

Ian Fleming and his wife, Anne, the former Lady Rothermere, whom
he married in 1952. *Wide World Photos.*

At his home near Ocho Rios, Jamaica, Fleming wrote many of his famous thrillers on a rigid work schedule which allowed him time to enjoy the climate and surroundings of his favorite retreat. *London Daily Express.*

The author clowns, on location in Turkey for the shooting of the film *From Russia, with Love*. A Turkish train, rented for the film, provides a menacing backdrop. *Wide World Photos*.

Left to right: Author Fleming, Producers Harry Saltzman and Albert R. Broccoli on the set for the filming of *Goldfinger*. *Pictorial Parade*.

an Connery portrays James Bond
the astonishingly successful films
sed on Fleming books, *Dr. No,
om Russia, with Love, Goldfin-
r*, and *Thunderball*, produced by
bert R. Broccoli and Harry Saltz-
n and released through United
tists.

A luncheon chat with Ursula Andress, one of the stars of *Dr. No*, on location in Jamaica during the making of the film, produced by Albert R. Broccoli and Harry Saltzman and released through United Artists.

The sentences were, for the English engineers, fairly light. (The Russians did not fare so well, and applying the law of averages and what we know about conditions in Soviet prisons in those years, it must be assumed that most of them perished during their sentences, which ranged from eighteen months to ten years.) One man, Gregory, was acquitted; three others, including Monkhouse, were expelled; and Thornton received a sentence of three years and Macdonald one of two years.

The foreign reaction to these sentences and to the whole course of the trial was severe. Great Britain immediately banned Soviet exports and stopped negotiating the extension of the current trade agreement. In the United States, which was then considering recognition of the USSR, the reaction was equally unfavorable. The Russians were evidently surprised by this. From their point of view, they had treated the accused leniently, and they overlooked the fact that it was the lack of a fair trial which aroused indignation. They either believed their own nonsense about class justice or else expected that the world would tolerantly go along with their ideas. In any event, the tough British attitude paid off, because the two men who had been imprisoned were released later in the same summer.

Ian Fleming, as the Reuters' staff man at the Metro-Vickers trial, had played an important part in keeping the world informed of the course of these proceedings and thus contributed to an understanding of the Soviet system. All this must have had a rather stimulating effect on the imagination of the man who was later to concern himself so greatly with intrigue. He had witnessed in action the peculiar Soviet concept of justice, he had seen with his own eyes the effect of OGPU treatment on recalcitrant witnesses, and he had heard with his own ears of the effectiveness of the nonviolent brainwashing which the Russians were then perfecting. He had heard one of the most vicious prosecuting attorneys in history in action; Vyshinsky was one of the few real men who could measure up to Fleming's own fictional villains. He had, in short, found a world where men accepted injustice as the ordinary course of life, and seen the accused Russians confess their way indifferently to death because they knew it was hopeless to simply say, "I have not done it. I am not guilty." Fleming came from an entirely different world, a world which proclaimed a conception of honor and duty for which his father had died. This look at another grimmer idea of life which was suddenly thrown into sharp conflict with treasured English conceptions of justice and truth must have made a deep impression.

Fleming did a good job of covering his first important story, and the opposition (INS) sent a telegram to Sir Roderick Jones reading: "SHOULD LIKE YOU TO KNOW THAT WE FELLOW JOURNALISTS OF IAN FLEMING WHO NONE OF US HAD EVER MET BEFORE HIS APPEARANCE HERE COVER MET-VICKERS TRIAL NOT ONLY CONSIDER HIM A PUKKHA CHAP PERSONALLY BUT HAVE AN EX-TREMELY HIGH OPINION OF HIS JOURNALISTIC ABILITY STOP HE HAS GIVEN ALL OF US A RUN FOR OUR MONEY."

In the fall of 1933, Fleming, after his success at the Metro-Vickers trial, was regarded as a coming man and in line for a promotion. Fleming recalled in later years: "I must have done fairly well because Sir Roderick offered me the job of assistant general manager in the Far East. . . . I had begun at £ 240 a year and I was then getting £ 300. So I asked him what my salary would be. In the tone of one offering sacks of gold he said £ 800. I knew I wouldn't be able to keep up with the Joneses of Singapore, so I declined. At the same time, it seemed to me that if the best promotion Reuters could offer wasn't going to bring in enough money the only thing to do was resign, so I did and went into the City to make money."

Fleming's recollection of this incident was not quite accurate, but he conveyed the essential features of the incident. He actually took some time considering Reuters' offer and then wrote Sir Roderick Jones:

Just a week after our conversation, when I was about to write and accept the post you offered me, a business man with whom I am only slightly acquainted asked me to see him and offered me what at first sight appeared to be a quite exceptional post in his firm of merchant bankers. The gist of the offer was that he himself intended shortly to retire and that he offered me his partnership in the firm after two years of learning the business.

Although the offer appeared too good to be true, I subsequently found that it was perfectly sincere and that the firm in question was one of the most successful and reliable in the city. A partnership would be quite remarkably remunerative and I would acquire before I was 30 a position which it is unusual to obtain before the age of 50, if at all.

Robert Fleming [his banker grandfather] and a director of Baring Brothers both urged me to accept the offer and, having regard to its quite exceptional nature and to the fact that it has been made in all sincerity, I am afraid that I have no alternative but to ask you to be kind enough to accept my resignation from Reuters.

Fleming went on to express his regret at being forced to make such a decision and thanked Sir Roderick for the opportunities he had been given. He said some of the same things in a letter to Rickatson-Hatt, which is somewhat more personal. There he wrote:

I enclose a copy of a letter I have just written to Sir Roderick. I can't say how sorry I am to have had to take this step and I can hardly bear the thought of leaving Reuters after the wonderful two years training you have given me. I really had hoped to make a big career in journalism after all the encouragement you have given me, and the idea of having to go and sit on an office stool for the rest of my life is all the worse compared with the marvellous time you have given me with Reuters. But however much I hate the idea, I really can't afford to miss this amazing offer which will mean the hell of a lot of money very soon. Its a beastly idea giving up all the fun of life for money, but I hope I shall be able to make a packet and then get out and come back into journalism from the other end. Anyway, the decision had to be made and I was pretty well pushed into it from all sides. I was assured it was the "right thing to do" for the sake of the family—so there it is.

I loathe the idea from nearly every point of view, and I shall hate leaving you and Reuters. But I'm afraid it has got to be done.

Please forgive me for repaying all your kindness and the wonderful two years you have given me in this rotten way.

The final note in the Reuters' file on Fleming is from Rickatson-Hatt to Sir Roderick and states: "Fleming confirmed that his mother was principally responsible for persuading him to accept the offer in the city."

Fleming came to value his experience with Reuters. He told an interviewer: "It was in Reuters that I learned to write fast and, above all, to be accurate, because in Reuters if you weren't accurate you were fired, and that was the end of that."

Ian Fleming did not make his fortune in the City. He was first with Cull and Company and then was a partner at Rowe and Pitman's, one of the great English stockbroking firms. But he said himself that he was "no good at it," although he enjoyed the life.

"Those financial firms are tremendous clubs," he said, "and great fun, but I never could figure out what a sixty-fourth of a point was. We used to spend our whole time throwing telephones at each other. I'm afraid we ragged far too much."

By 1939 Fleming was "rather fed up" with making a fortune in the City and when *The Times* offered him a job as special correspondent accompanying a trade mission to Moscow, he jumped at the chance.

This assignment was by no means as interesting as his previous coverage of the Metro-Vickers affair, but it gave him an excellent opportunity to form an estimate of the menacing atmosphere in Europe at that time. In fact, Fleming's assignment was more or less elbowed out of *The Times* by Hitler's seizing the remainder of Czechoslovakia and threatening Poland. The matter of getting the Russians to buy English, which had looked important to both the Foreign Office and *The Times* when the mission was contemplated, played second fiddle to more sinister maneuvers.

Fleming noted this in his first dispatch from Moscow on March 23rd. He wrote: "The political situation has naturally overshadowed the commercial talks for which Mr. Hudson's visit was planned, and, although the latter will continue as intended, it is understood that the preliminary exchange of views dealt largely with wider questions. In this connexion it is believed that the response of the Soviet authorities to the latest British *démarche* has been guardedly favourable. It is also thought that there have been hurried consultations between Moscow and Warsaw during the past 48 hours with a view to stiffening the morale of the Baltic States."

The following day the head of the mission, Mr. Hudson, the Secretary for Overseas Trade, met with Mikoyan, who was then Commissar for Foreign Trade. Fleming, in his report, again noted the ominous atmosphere in Europe and said: "It is realized that there are other factors which will at the moment weigh heavily with both parties, and it is presumed that the present community of interests between the two Governments may lead to a more rapid settlement of outstanding trade differences than might have been the case in other circumstances."

After the formal talks, the mission engaged in certain ceremonial activities, and it is interesting to see that Fleming paid close attention to the security precautions of the Soviets. When the Embassy car went into the Kremlin through a medieval gateway, Fleming noted that the gate was "heavily reinforced with armour-plating," and that the car entered "to the accompaniment of the flashing green lights and clanging alarm bells which are part of the installation designed to deter uninvited guests." On leaving the Kremlin, Fleming observed that the guests passed into Red Square "through a sliding bombproof doorway."

Fleming returned to London late in March and the possibility of war became ever more likely. Then Fleming "began to hear funny little questions being asked about me; friends would tell me that so-and-so had been asking about where had I been, what did I know, and so on." These funny little questions eventually turned into an offer that was to determine Fleming's career for the next six years, and which in turn played a great part in the writing of the Bond books.

CHAPTER

3

A Good War

THE people asking questions about Fleming were from Naval Intelligence. They needed a man who had "good languages and some knowledge of The City" and Fleming had been recommended to them by the governor of The Bank of England and the head of Baring Brothers, a large firm of merchant bankers; he seemed to fill the bill. The upshot of it was that Fleming was invited to lunch at the Carlton Hotel by Admiral John H. Godfrey "and a couple of other very quiet characters in plain clothes," and when the lunch was over Fleming was asked to join the Navy as Personal Assistant to Admiral Godfrey, who was Director of Naval Intelligence. He was given a commission as lieutenant in the Royal Naval Volunteer Reserve and went to work at the Admiralty.

Fleming liked and respected Admiral Godfrey, who in many ways served as the model for "M" in the later Bond novels. Godfrey was a remarkable officer according to those who knew him best. Tall and broad-shouldered, he had a reputation as one of the best navigators in the Fleet, and yet he more closely resembled a prosecuting attorney than an old sea dog. When cross-examining a subordinate, his habitual frown often gave way to a steely grin that left strong men weak and perspiring by the time the interview was over.

Godfrey quickly recruited a formidable array of unconventional talent to provide the Navy with intelligence about Axis operations. It was a job that badly needed doing but for which the British were ill-prepared. At the start of the war, years of neglect had weakened this particular branch of the Navy, and Fleming and his Admiral were aware that they would have to work like titans to repair the damage done by years of idleness.

The Admiral assembled a battery of lawyers, college professors, reporters, industrial designers, geologists and geographers, put them into harness with Royal Navy Commanders and Royal Marine Majors, and demanded immediate results. Fleming was the link between Godfrey and all the multitudinous activities of the department, which ranged through cracking codes, setting up bizarre false scents for the other side to trip over, preparing maps of enemy-occupied territory, interrogating spies and training British agents. Fleming had to know and report to Admiral Godfrey what all these assorted branches were up to every hour of the day.

In the early days of the war they had a number of embarrassing moments, for though it was soon apparent what the principal weaknesses in Naval Intelligence were, it took some time to take the necessary steps to assemble a smoothly operating and efficient department. In particular, the Royal Navy suffered from a lack of reconnaisance aircraft which could keep it informed of the movements of the enemy, one of the major tasks of any naval intelligence unit. The sea is a vast battlefield and it is vital to keep oneself informed of the disposition of the enemy's forces, so as to assemble a superior force of one's own to attack him. The British, throughout World War II, enjoyed numerical superiority to the German surface fleet, but in the early days of the war an inadequate knowledge of where the enemy was concentrating his forces led to some bad times.

The invasion of Norway was in many respects the Royal Navy's darkest hour, and it was mainly due to a failure of intelligence. If the fleet had had adequate knowledge of the German movements, it could have used its strength to either deny them passage to Norway or else to make this passage very costly. Here, the problem was not entirely one of lack of intelligence, for the movements of the Germans did not pass unnoticed, but more one of either ignoring or misinterpreting this information. The Admiralty was always afraid that the German pocket battleships and cruisers would break out into the Atlantic and play havoc with the convoys coming from the United States and Canada which kept England supplied, so that when the movements were observed the response was to try to deny the Germans access to the North Atlantic instead of moving in to prevent them from approaching Norway. There were only a few hours in which to take preventive measures, and this invaluable time was lost because the intelligence about the enemy's movements was badly misinterpreted.

This mistake got Naval Intelligence such a bad reputation that later, during the period when Hitler was preparing for the invasion of England, many destroyers were drawn away from their normal duty of protecting convoys in the North Atlantic to stand by in order to deny the English Channel to the anticipated invaders. This showed a total lack of confidence in intelligence, for such a massive operation should normally be expected to be spotted, even by an inefficient Naval Intelligence, over 24 hours in advance, and the destroyers should have been left on convoy patrol until that time. Again, this deployment proved costly, for the U-boats racked up large scores among the unprotected merchant shipping.

Still, the intelligence provided for the Navy continued to be woefully lacking. After the fall of Norway an unusual concentration of enemy warships, including battle cruisers and cruisers, were brought together in Trondheim fjord for a period of six weeks; this was never correctly reported. No wonder Admiral Forbes lamented in an official report: "It is most galling that the enemy should know just where our ships . . . always are, whereas we generally learn where his major forces are when they sink one or more of our ships."

Obviously, Fleming and Godfrey had their work cut out for them as the war began. Fleming was squarely in the center of all the muddle and his position was far from an easy one. Godfrey often used him as liaison with other services and departments in the Navy, and there must have been trying days when these people felt that Naval Intelligence was letting them down. In addition, Fleming was expected to ride herd on the men who were slowly shaking down to an effective team; he often had to demand results from them before they were well settled into their jobs.

It was particularly galling to Fleming to be an administrator, sending men out to perform deeds of daring that he genuinely longed to tackle himself. He sat at a corner desk six feet from the door, and within his purview came every visitor, every file, every barrage of questions from the always inquisitive Godfrey, and every reply from the harried staff.

The Department of Naval Intelligence was known as N.I.D. 17, and Fleming signed all his correspondence 17F. The Department was located in Room 39 of the Old Admiralty, and with Fleming in the room were others of Godfrey's staff—a stockbroker, a lawyer, two Royal Navy captains, a paymaster and a confidential secretary.

From his window, Fleming could see straight across the Horse Guards Parade to Number 10 Downing Street and the Foreign Office, the dual centers of Great Britain's wartime activity. Across this gravel square Fleming could watch the comings and goings of the head of the Secret Service, the General in Charge of S.O.E. (experts on sabotage and resistance) and the various Chiefs of Staff.

At that time Fleming was in some ways the image of James Bond. He was in his early thirties and had a long, sad face with cleanly etched features and very clear blue eyes. He moved gracefully and with determination. After the war a friend of those years (and a Bond fan) suggested that all men see themselves as a perpetual 28 or 30, and Fleming replied, *"Touché."* Yet he never got to play an active part in the war, aside from a stint as observer at the Dieppe raid and various trips with Admiral Godfrey. He used to complain of getting corns on his backside from so much sitting.

Yet, sitting at his desk, Fleming played an important role in the British war effort. He introduced Sefton Delmer, whom he had known before the war, to Godfrey, and Godfrey resolved to use him as an agent in Lisbon. Before this was possible, Delmer became involved in the operation of a "black" radio station directed at Germany. Briefly, the idea of "black" radio was to direct a barrage of the dirtiest kind of propaganda at the enemy in the hopes of breaking his morale. It was distinguished from "white" radio in that Great Britain took no official responsibility for what was said over it, so that lies and deceptions could be perpetrated which were not possible for the BBC. Black radio, for example, often pretended to be a station operating from Germany or German occupied territory, so that its statements would be received by listeners, not as coming from the enemy, but as emanating from their own government.

Fleming saw the value this kind of operation might have for Naval Intelligence and it was a simple matter for him to convince Godfrey. Delmer had always wanted to operate a station aimed at the German armed forces, and now he was given his chance. The station was called *Atlantik-sender,* and Delmer operated it in conjunction with Donald McLachlan and Robert Harling, who were members of Godfrey's staff.

Atlantiksender purported to be run by the German Navy to provide entertainment and news for their personnel at sea and in foreign naval stations. Delmer assembled a mixed staff of English staff officers and Germans who had decided that Hitler was not for them. In colloquial German, the station operated on a formula of mixing a heavy proportion of cover stories with occasional bits of dirt. The cover stories came from the usual official German sources and Atlantiksender even broadcast speeches by Goebbels and Hitler, while dirt was often a fact twisted slightly or a whole-cloth fabrication which nevertheless had an air of probability to it.

Fleming followed the work of Atlantiksender, and he must have been often amused and always intrigued by its antics, particularly those which were directly calculated to break down the morale of the German Navy. Atlantiksender reported in great detail the raids on German cities, even going so far as to list the names of streets which had been damaged. This greatly impressed the German listeners, for the reports were generally accurate, and even those who knew that Atlantiksender was a British propaganda outlet listened for these details. Many Germans believed, because of the authenticity of this information, that Atlantiksender had agents throughout Germany feeding them this and other information. The truth was somewhat simpler. Delmer's staff received reports from the R.A.F., including pictures taken by a reconnaissance plane minutes after a bombing was over, and from this was able to prepare an accurate picture of the bombing after the planes returned to their bases.

Atlantiksender also had a highly desirable effect on German naval prisoners. Naval Intelligence agents in Europe sent back such trivial bits of information as the results of soccer games between U-boat crews, and when these were broadcast over Atlantiksender, the U-boat men became convinced that the British knew all the details of their lives.

When they were interrogated, many said, "The British know everything already. I might as well talk and make things a little easier for myself."

Another element that contributed to this effect was Atlantiksender's habit of playing special request music for U-boat crews which had just left on a long voyage. Hearing this, the U-boat men became despondent at the thought that all their rigorous security precautions were of no value, for no sooner were they at sea than Atlantiksender was serenading them. Actually, these hits were no more than inspired guesswork on the part of Naval Intelligence, which had some idea of the movement of individual U-boats, but by no means had it down to an exact science.

A similar instance arose in the case of a German Luftwaffe commander who was shot down at sea and willingly provided quantities of information because he had become convinced by an Atlantiksender broadcast that British Naval Intelligence knew all there was to know. What had happened was that the Navy had spotted five vessels in the Gironde estuary which they assumed were blockade runners. To get on the men's nerves, they played some special request music for them and then followed this up with an account of the objections the Luftwaffe were raising to providing air cover to these ships.

In this instance, Atlantiksender guessed exactly right. The Luftwaffe commander had raised exactly these objections. He went back to his quarters, turned on Atlantiksender and, hearing his own views over the enemy station, naturally assumed that his meeting with the blockade runners had been bugged. When he was captured shortly after, he reasoned that if Atlantiksender could report a briefing minutes

after it had been held, there was nothing much he could
tell British Naval Intelligence that it didn't already know.

One of black radio's more spectacular successes involved
the Italian fleet. After the invasion of Italy, Radio Livorno
was set up to induce the Italian Navy to surrender to the
Allies. Pretending to operate from an Italian warship at
Livorno, the station continually warned against German
attempts to seize the Italian fleet. Then, it gradually became
apparent that Livorno was negotiating a surrender of the
Italian Navy to Admiral Cunningham. Finally, on Septem-
ber 10, 1943, Radio Livorno ordered the Italian Navy to
surrender to the Allies at Malta, and the Italian ships put to
sea and obediently surrendered. Actually, the commanding
Italian officers had long since known that Radio Livorno
was broadcasting under the orders of Admiral Cunningham
and had surrendered because the terms offered were acceptable to them; nevertheless, black radio had been used as an
instrument in communicating with the Italians and had
played an important role in effecting their surrender.

By this point in the war, Naval Intelligence had come a
long way since its low point during the invasion of Norway.
Agents had been recruited, aerial reconnaissance pinpointed
enemy shipping, monitors kept German radio traffic under
constant surveillance, and other technical devices, such as
radar and sonar, had been introduced to quickly detect
German U-boats. By 1943 Admiral Doenitz was lamenting:
"The enemy knows all our secrets and we know none of
his." Putting together an organization from scratch that
effectively informed the Admiralty of the enemy's every
move was a remarkable achievement for Godfrey and his
personal assistant, Ian Fleming.

The secret war for Fleming was not all well-drilled organization and cold administration. It had its comic opera moments. Fleming once had the notion that he could obtain valuable secret information from the captured navigator and captain of a U-boat on how they had avoided the British minefields in the Skagerrak if he wined and dined them sufficiently. He took them out of the prison camp, together with a British officer from the submarine service and, after a day's sightseeing in London, brought them to Scott's, a posh Piccadilly restaurant. All concerned drank and ate heartily while Fleming talked about the sea to his German "brothers" and sympathized with them about being forced to fight by the wicked politicians.

While this was going on, one of the waiters became suspicious of the entire set-up and tipped off Scotland Yard. Fleming arrived back at his office and, after tipsily reporting that he had not learned a thing about the Germans in the Skagerrak, received a dressing down from Godfrey, who icily informed him that the only result of his sortie was to mobilize half the detectives in Scotland Yard to investigate the suspicious dinner party at Scott's.

On another occasion, Intelligence was asked to help prepare the Arabs for the American invasion of North Africa. They used a shifty little man named Mohammed Ali, who happened to be a tea merchant. They agreed with Mohammed Ali that one of the best methods of smoothing the path of the Allied armies would be to prepare millions of leaflets explaining the benefits of the Allied rule, whereupon Mohammed Ali wrote out a dandy little slogan and had the leaflets printed. They were then duly showered on the natives by the R.A.F.

One morning shortly thereafter, an American officer pounded on the door of the Arab section of Naval Intelligence and demanded, "Do you know what this is?"

"Of course, old boy," was the reply. "It's our leaflet. Explains things to the Arabs and all that. We've dropped millions of them."

"But do you know what it says?" asked the American.

"Certainly. 'All Mohammedans must support the Allies.' "

"It does not," came the icy rejoinder. "It says, 'Buy Mohammed Ali's green tea.' "

In 1940, a letter addressed to the Minister of Home Defence came into the possession of the Joint Intelligence Committee. It had supposedly been written by a German agent who had been sent into the country a year or two earlier, along with a number of German refugees. After spending some time in England, he had become so enamored of the qualities of English life that he could no longer bear the thought of betraying them to the Nazis, though he still considered himself a loyal German.

He described in minute detail the preparations for an attack by a battalion of German paratroops at Southend, an English seaside resort. The letter appeared to be authentic. Mistakes in grammar and spelling were of the sort a recent arrival from Germany would make. The "spy" knew about the tides, which were very important to paratroops landing on the beach. The sentiments the converted Anglophile pleaded as justification for betraying his own cause also seemed credible. The letter was taken seriously and preparations were made to give the German paratroops a hostile reception.

Fleming, in due course, heard about all this and pointed

out that since the attack was scheduled for Sunday, valuable time would be lost in giving an account of the battle, which was bound to be widely played up in the press, to the anxiously awaiting world. In this time the Germans could and would say anything they pleased about the situation. Some provision must be made for the preparation of an authentic report of the British triumph at Southend, without endangering security.

Impressed by this reasoning, the Joint Intelligence Committee sent Fleming and a companion bowling down to Southend in a camouflaged staff car, with all the credentials necessary to act as official eyewitnesses and report this great battle for posterity.

All this took place during Britain's darkest hour, shortly after Dunkirk, when there was good reason for expecting a German attack. Arriving in Southend on a Bank Holiday weekend, Fleming found the place in a surprisingly festive mood. Couples strolled the boardwalk, bands played in hotel lounges, and long lines formed outside of cinema houses. The air did not seem heavy with menace.

Moving about the countryside, Fleming found some gunners at Shoeburyness who didn't have any guns, a lonely Lewis gun protruding from the bandstand of a long pier, and, as dusk fell, a scattering of men from the Pioneer Corps who had been remustered after Dunkirk and didn't seem to know who their officers were. Wondering whether to laugh or cry, Fleming joined a party of naval officers on the roof of a hotel and anxiously peered out to sea, while from the ballroom below the strains of "The Lambeth Walk" and "South of the Border" wafted to them.

As the night wore on, the whole mission began to seem

farcical, and after one o'clock, when no unusual air activity had been reported, Fleming and his companion returned to their car, piled their drunken driver into the back seat, and returned to London. Fleming, in later years, often wondered who had written the letter which started all the fuss; Fleming had found his match at creating fictional suspense.

In 1941, after the battle of Crete, Fleming was given his most interesting assignment in Naval Intelligence. At Crete the Germans had sent on with their advance units an operational intelligence unit whose sole job was to seize intelligence data at British forward headquarters, make an on-the-spot evaluation of what they obtained, and then send it back to Germany. This German unit was extremely successful. Admiral Godfrey determined to create a British unit based on this German model, and he placed Fleming in charge.

The unit was designated Number 30 Assault Unit, or 30 AU, and it began to operate in the Middle East, working in conjunction with the Eighth Army. The field commanders were Quintin Riley, a one-time Polar explorer, and Dunstan Curtis, who had been educated as a lawyer. The Lords of the Admiralty were slow to recognize the value of this unit, which they deemed highly irregular, but when word of German intelligence techniques began coming back from North Africa, Sicily and Italy, they were happy to change their opinion.

Thirty AU was, in effect, a private army, and the men in it liked it immensely, combining as it did all the thrills of piracy with an absence of military discipline. As preparations were being made for D-day in Europe, the unit was withdrawn from the south and brought back to England, where Fleming could directly supervise its activities.

By this time, Fleming was serving under a new Director of Naval Intelligence, Rear-Admiral Rushbrooke, a tall, intellectual type who was less inclined to adventure than Godfrey. He sometimes seemed alarmed at 30 AU's antics, but was unable to gainsay the results.

Fleming divided 30 AU into two sections, Royal Navy and Royal Marines. The Marines were to do any fighting necessary to get at the information desired and the Navy was to collect and evaluate it. The Marines were a collection of cocky, courageous, amoral, lying rascals who performed their duties well in battle but were inclined to go chasing women and strong drink the minute action was over.

After D-day, 30 AU performed valuable service in obtaining technical knowledge of U-boat construction, torpedo performance and German electronic equipment by rushing in and grabbing it in the midst of the battle for Europe. The unit also had its incidental heroes, one of whom captured a complete German radar setup with three hundred men by insisting, in halting German, that he had the place covered with heavy artillery when he actually only had a half-dozen men with him. Another, while entering the U-boat pens at Cherbourg, was shot through his open mouth, which, while it did him little permanent physical damage, ruined his hard-earned reputation as a tight-lipped man of action.

The unit also had its share of characters who sometimes drove Fleming frantic. There was one man completely without nerves whose idea of kicks was to commandeer a jeep and drive around no-man's-land dodging shellfire. There was also a bomb-disposal ace who insisted that he had no knowledge of mechanical things and proved it by getting himself stranded when his jeep slipped a fanbelt. Fleming also had to contend with a diver who always popped back to the surface after inspecting a sunken sub just in time to rendezvous with the brandy and soda his current girl friend was preparing.

Still more aggravating, and more important to Fleming, was the fact that he was expected to control half a dozen highly individualistic splinter groups which were wandering all over the map of Europe on a treasure hunt for German intelligence data. He proved to be patient and long-suffering with his often unruly subordinates, and composed long, explanatory letters to them explaining their tasks, and, when necessary, explosive rockets to get them back to concentrating on their military duties. Again, he was the middle man between the unit's men in the field and the Admiralty experts who told him what to look for. It was up to him to translate their requirements into operational orders which could be followed by the men of 30 AU.

He did this job almost too well, for the success of 30 AU was such that it was noticed by the higher brass and his private army was finally absorbed into the larger T-force under SHAEF and General Eisenhower.

Before this happened, Fleming wangled a few trips to Europe to inspect conditions in the field. On one of these, he found it necessary to ask General Patton for permission for 30 AU to operate with Patton's army. Patton was a great actor and, in addition to granting Fleming's request, favored him with a vivid account of how the war would be won. Later, Fleming and Robert Harlach, a member of 30 AU, stopped by the roadside to gobble a few cans of Spam and wash them down with a bottle of Calvados someone had commandeered. After Patton's stirring speech and the brandy, the war seemed almost over, and Harlach asked Fleming what he was going to do when that happy day arrived. Fleming replied: "I shall write the spy story to end all spy stories." Harlach wrote, "I almost choked on my Spam."

The war gave Fleming a unique insight into the techniques of espionage. He knew, for example, that Naval Intelligence had sent a false priest to hear confession from a U-boat captain so as to trick him into giving knowledge that was vital to save British seamen. (Later, the U-boat captain claimed he realized a trick was being played on him, but wanted to give the information and had been glad to do it in such a way that his conscience was salved.)

He knew that when the Russians sent two Bulgars to assassinate Franz von Papen in Ankara, they gave one a blue case and the other a red one. The Russians told the assassins that the red case contained a bomb which was to be thrown at von Papen while the blue case contained a smoke bomb which would conceal their getaway when a button was pressed. The bomb was to be thrown, then the smoke released.

The Bulgars decided to better their chances by releasing the smoke first. This decision saved von Papen's life, for both cases contained bombs, and the Bulgars were demolished while von Papen was only knocked down by the impact of the explosion. The Russians had decided to eliminate the assassins once their mission was accomplished and thought up a rather neat way to do it. Fleming later made use of this situation in *Casino Royale,* along with his own ill-fated gambling experience in Lisbon related at the beginning of this book.

In fact, all of this wartime background was utilized, in one way or another, in his later work. He said: "I couldn't possibly have had a more exciting or interesting War. Of course, it's my experience in Naval Intelligence, and what I learned about secret operations of one sort or another, that finally led me to write about them—in a highly bowdlerized way—with James Bond as the central figure."

After the war Fleming maintained his interest in all kinds of espionage. When he was writing the Bond books, he met and liked Allen Dulles and the two often discussed intelligence operations. While he thought of the Bond novels as diversions from the cares of the day, he thought that real espionage was a deadly serious business. He told Dulles: "It's all-out war! People who raise questions about ethics, moral standards, that sort of thing, just don't understand what it's about. I mean the head of the CIA and his opposite number in Russia, in this case Semichastney, head of Soviet State Security—they are absolutely like two commanders in chief in the field! I mean, all right—you see the traffic in the streets and everything's quiet and orderly here. But these two men have been locked in deadly combat— for years!"

When the war was won, Ian Fleming returned to his first love, journalism. Lord Kemsley made him foreign manager for his chain of papers, the principal one being *The Sunday Times* of London (which has no connection with *The Times* of London). He stayed in this position until 1959, by which time the Kemsley chain had been absorbed by the Thomson newspapers. A colleague recalled him at policy conferences, "brimming with ideas, consistent only in his opposition to sham and stuffed-shirt attitudes, generous in his praise and devastating in his blame, laughing uproariously when something appealed to his highly developed sense of the ridiculous. He was . . . an Etonian radical of journalism, striving all the time to see that the whole truth was told."

Fleming enjoyed his newspaper work, but somewhere at the back of his mind the fascination of the life he had seen during the war continued to grow, and in 1952 a crisis in his personal life brought all this material spinning to the surface.

CHAPTER

4

Author at Work

THE *Daily Express* for February 8, 1952, announced: "Viscount Rothermere was granted a decree *nisi* in the divorce court yesterday. Lady Rothermere did not defend a charge of misconduct with Mr. Ian Lancaster Fleming, who was ordered to pay all costs." Ian Fleming did what any gentleman would do in such a case; on March 25, 1952, *The Times* announced the marriage of Ian Fleming and the former Lady Rothermere.

Anne Fleming was not the only woman in Fleming's life. Fleming had known a good many women before his marriage and, like many habitual bachelors, was interested in the opposite sex but wary of lasting attachments. Someone said, "Ian is like a handful of sea water; he slips away through your fingers—even while you're watching."

He admitted to Susan Barnes of *The Sunday Express* having had an affair with a bubble dancer. He defined a bubble dancer as "someone who leaps around the stage with very little on and a huge balloon while *The Flight of the Bumblebee* is being played."

The affair didn't turn out too well, according to Fleming, although the lady "was a rather spiffing girl called Storm. But the whole affair was very unsatisfactory. When the public performance was over, it was always the same old thing: 'I'm sorry, darling, but I'm too tired. I've got to appear at the Embassy tomorrow night.' Unless you can further their careers, these actors and actresses really aren't interested."

He also complained of American women who "are sometimes too obsessed with cleanliness and bugs and so on.

"I had an affair with an American girl once—before I was married—and right after I had finished kissing her she insisted on gargling with TCP in case she'd caught something."

He also had complaints about Englishwomen. "Englishwomen are absolutely filthy. Any hairdresser will tell you that. They think that putting on more make-up is enough.

"Mark you, I'm comparing them to the Japanese and American women. They know that just to lie in a bath and stew is no way to get clean. The Japanese wash themselves first and afterwards get into a large communal bath where they sit happily and talk with their friends. They would never think of lying in their own effluvia."

A Fleet Street colleague wrote that Fleming's bachelor days "included spirited encounters with bubble-dancers and baronesses," said that he had "firm views on women," and told the following anecdote:

"I reminded him of an evening we spent together in Istanbul, the highlight of which was a belly-dancer whose quivering navel dislodged the fine ash off the end of his Balkan cigarette.

" 'You observed at the time,' I said, 'that busts no longer were the most beautiful feature of a woman's figure, but that the buttocks most certainly were.'

" 'Nor have I changed my mind,' Fleming replied."

Fleming did not care for "the slinky vampire type, fashion models, actresses. You could only conceivably think that they are sexy if you've no experience of them. They are always so frightened of getting bruised or bent in any way —because it would upset their careers."

He preferred undemanding, helpful women; he said, when asked about his ideal woman, "I think I very much like the WREN type of woman. . . . I like the fact that they seem to want to please, to make one happy." But he also admitted, "In the end, one ends up marrying entirely the opposite of what one thinks, you know, which I have done."

Fleming married after what Robert Harlach, who knew both parties, describes as "a period of shattering personal complexities and tensions for himself and his wife, experiences which would have meant nervous breakdowns for lesser combatants." Anne Fleming was definitely not the WREN type. Harlach describes her as "a slim, dark, handsome, highly strung, iconoclastic creature of middle height with a fine pair of flashpoint eyes. She has something of the air of an imperious gypsy." She was one of London's leading hostesses who gave frequent dinner parties enlivened by good food, good wine, and highly intellectual men given to passionate exposition of opposed points of view.

She had a talent for stimulating brilliant men and revelled in the company of a long list of England's most brilliant minds, who naturally appreciated her ability to bring out the best in them. Guests at her parties have included Somerset Maugham, Evelyn Waugh, Sir Isaiah Berlin (philosopher), Sir Maurice Bowra (classical scholar), Sir Frederick Ashton (choreographer), Cecil Beaton (photographer), Malcolm Muggeridge, Noel Coward, Randolph Churchill, Lucian Freud, Peter Quennell (poet and historian), and Cyril Connolly.

Anne Fleming was interested in the saber-like displays of male wit, and this interest plus the rough edge of her own tongue sometimes provoked somewhat reserved responses in members of her own sex. She did have a number of close female friends, however, including Lady Avon (the wife of Anthony Eden), Lady Diana Duff Cooper, and Loelia, Duchess of Westminster.

Fleming had no particular liking for his wife's dinner parties. He said: "What happens if I attend a dinner party in my own house is that all the interesting men are placed by Annie at her end of the table and I get stuck at the bottom of the table with the less interesting wives who are craning their necks to hear what Annie and the interesting men are saying instead of listening to my stammer." He often spent the evenings on which they took place at the Portland Club, playing bridge for high stakes. Returning at midnight, he often found the guests still embroiled in assorted literary and political discussions; he merely waved a distant greeting and proceeded upstairs to his own room.

The marriage survived one of its rockier moments when Fleming came home one night to find Cyril Connolly reading page proofs of the first Bond book aloud to the assembled multitude with heavily theatrical emphasis which the guests evidently found amusing. Anne was no great admirer of her husband's literary endeavors. "These dreadful Bond books," she called them publicly. Still, she relished their later success and the preview of *Dr. No* gave her an opportunity to involve Somerset Maugham and other literati in a whirlwind of festivities.

Malcolm Muggeridge, who was not exactly a fan of the Bond books, was sometimes present at Anne Fleming's soirées. But he found it "more congenial to talk with him [Fleming] about Fleet Street gossip and newspaper circulations than to join in the, as I thought, rather dismal conversational free-for-all which surged endlessly around Anne." He, too, would climb out of the din and join Fleming in "a sort of private apartment at the top of the house where he kept his golf clubs, pipes and other masculine bric-a-brac. We would sit up there together sipping a highball; like climbers taking a breather above a mountain torrent whose roar could still faintly be heard in the ravine below."

When they were first married, Fleming moved out of his own bachelor mews house in Mayfair, and Anne, of course, left Rothermere's mansion, Warwick House, overlooking the Green Park. They moved into a large Chelsea flat overlooking the Thames. The flat, view of the river and all, did not seem to be in the right style for Anne Fleming, and they soon moved to a Regency, cream-stuccoed house in Victoria Square (London's smallest square), situated only about a hundred yards from the riding school of Buckingham Palace.

The house is a charming example of English urban architecture, and was particularly well adapted to the requirements of both Flemings. There was a bowed dining room which could seat eight in comfort but frequently took on a dozen or more to accommodate Anne's talking dinner parties.

Built on a corner, with emphatically bowed windows, the house had a warm, welcoming air, the result of a carefully designed "casual" throwing together of comfortable chairs and sofas, Regency furniture, Fleming's black Wedgwood busts, numerous books, and a somewhat eccentric collection of paintings by Augustus John, Lucian Freud and lesser Victorian daubers, rounded off by brass pictures of giddy goddesses and long-forgotten martial heroes.

The Fleming household included their son, Caspar, now 12, who Anne felt was destined to become Prime Minister; Fleming seemed to prefer a somewhat less prominent position for his son. Caspar was aware of his father's popularity. Fleming told an interviewer, "He doesn't read me, but he sells my autographs for seven shillings a time."

Anne Fleming had a son and a daughter by her first marriage to Baron O'Neill, who was killed in World War II. The son, now over thirty, is the fourth Baron and runs his estate in Northern Ireland and a garage in Belfast, while his sister, Fiona, is married to a young Foreign Office First Secretary.

The comparison of the literary-social world in which Anne Fleming moved and her husband's somewhat quieter existence may give the wrong impression of Fleming. He also enjoyed people and in his own way was as social as anybody; it was just that the people he was interested in were not always the same people his wife liked.

A friend in New York publishing recalls that he was a

good drinking companion who enjoyed parties and people. He knew writers, journalists, bureaucrats and bartenders and took a genuine interest in all of them. He made lasting friendships and was not one for mere casual acquaintance. He only asked that people should not bore him; if they succeeded in enlisting his interest, he stayed interested. Toward the end of his life when he was lionized throughout the Western world, and could have been seen with anyone he chose, he kept in close touch with the friends he had made when he was not so well known. He was interested in his friends' jobs and careers and often gave sound advice on how to prosper in the world.

"He had a shrewd mind," one man recalled. "He knew what made things tick. He was at the same time both tough-minded and romantic, in the sense that he was really interested in things and never cynical. He wasn't an angle-player and he never lost the fun of things.

"He was fun to be with. He lived hard and played hard and threw himself passionately into everything he did. People liked him enormously. He was one of the kindest men I've ever known and very generous."

Sometime in 1951 Ian Fleming was having lunch with William Plomer and asked him how one got cigarette smoke out of a woman once one had got it in. He explained that he didn't like "exhaled" or "puffed it out." Plomer looked at him sharply and said, "You've written a book."

Fleming had, indeed, written a book. The thought of his then imminent marriage alarmed Fleming. He said, "Horrified by the prospect of marriage and to anesthetize my nerves, I sat down, rolled a piece of paper into my battered portable and began." The book he wrote was *Casino Royale,* and the promise he had made, probably half-jokingly, during the war was fulfilled.

Fleming wrote *Casino Royale,* as he did all his later books, at his Jamaican retreat, Goldeneye. "When I got back to London," he wrote later, "I did nothing with the manuscript. I was too ashamed of it. No publisher would want it, and, if one did, I would not have the face to see it in print." Then he had lunch with Plomer, confessed his crime, and showed him the manuscript, feeling that Plomer would "tell the horrible truth about the book without condemning me or being scornful." Plomer read *Casino Royale,* liked it, and persuaded Fleming to pass it on to a publisher. The rest is an important part of the history of pop art in the twentieth century (which we will cover later in this chapter).

Fleming, like many other writers who accomplish a fairly substantial body of work, was a great believer in routine. He wrote the first draft of all his novels in Jamaica and, in doing so, kept regular hours at a writing desk far removed from the temptations and worries of his ordinary existence in London. He professed to think of himself as lazy and said his heart sank when he looked at two or three hundred blank sheets of paper which had to be filled in order to complete one of the Bond books.

To get around this, he deliberately created a vacuum in his life which could only be filled by some form of creative work. So he went every year to the house he had built in Jamaica in 1946, just after the war.

He had spent some time during the war in the Caribbean devising means of coping with the U-boat sinkings in the area, and he "loved every minute of it." He'd never been in the tropics before and thought they were wonderful. He was determined at the time to come back and build a house, and when the war was over he did just that.

He borrowed a car from a former associate in Naval Intelligence and found a donkey's racecourse by the sea which was not being used, bought it, and built on it a house he designed himself in London while the V-1's and V-2's were falling.

Goldeneye was located near the little banana port of Orcabassa. The name came from an operation which involved Fleming during the war: Operation Goldeneye was a detailed plan for the defense of Gibraltar in case it was attacked by the Spanish. Fleming had been reading Carson McCullers' *Reflections in a Golden Eye* about the time he bought the property, and it reminded him of the name. He had thought of calling the house Shamelady, after a Jamaican plant whose leaves curl up when they are touched. The first time he saw the plot he had looked over the edge of a cliff and found "the most beautiful naked Negress" bathing in the waves, and since the whole thirty acres were covered with this particular plant, the idea had a certain appeal. But in the end he decided this was "a little bit too fancy."

To write the Bond books, Fleming went to Jamaica every year during January and February, and sometimes stayed on until March. He got up every morning at half-past seven and then went for a swim, nude, in the ocean. He and his wife swam a hundred yards or so and then came back to a breakfast of scrambled eggs made by his Negro housekeeper, Violet. After breakfast he sat around in the garden accumulating ultra-violet rays until ten o'clock.

He then went to his bedroom and banged out 1,500 words in two and a half to three hours. He always had a rough idea of where he was going, but he never looked back at what he had done the day before. He never worried about mistakes and only tried to keep the narrative driving straight ahead. He claimed that if he looked back in mid-course, he would be lost, and said that if he had interrupted himself to have a look at what he had been doing, he would have been disgusted with himself and lucky to do five hundred words a day. At this point he never even checked facts or spelling, leaving all this until the book was completed.

After his morning's work, he jumped back into the ocean with a snorkel and spear and poked around the reefs for a while, sometimes catching an odd lobster or two but mostly just contemplating the marine life. He genuinely enjoyed this sport, and some of his best descriptive writing in the novels deals with this strange world under the waves.

Then he went back to the house for lunch, which he described as "a couple of pink gins" and "ordinary Jamaican food," but which very much impressed a reporter from *The Daily Express* who came to visit him, consisting as it did of such delicacies as curried goat, salamagundi (a mixture of raw herring, onions and spices), sailfish, *achee* (a local fruit, delicious when ripe, but a violent poison if eaten too early), fresh limes, grapefruit and pawpaw.

After lunch he napped from about half-past two until four, then went for another swim and returned to work about six. He worked for another hour, until it got dark, then numbered all the pages done that day and placed them neatly in a folder. For a reward, he mixed himself a couple of strong drinks, then went to dinner. After dinner he might go out for the evening to a neighbor's or stay at home playing Scrabble with his wife. He never drank seriously while he was doing a book, because he greatly believed in sticking to the routine and it worked. After two months of this regular but far from unpleasant existence, he had a finished Bond book in the folder.

He was not a particularly finicky writer. Aside from never correcting anything as he went along, he spent only a week or so going over the first draft "correcting the most glaring errors" before he sent the manuscript off to a typist. After getting it back, he worked on it a little bit, then sent it off to the publisher.

He appreciated having people point out either stylistic or factual mistakes to him and always had William Plomer read the finished manuscript. Fleming found that he would sometimes go through periods when he used one word much too frequently, and if he didn't catch this himself, he wanted someone to point it out before it was in print. One time Plomer said half-teasingly that though characters in one of the books often made exclamatory remarks, Fleming had not used any exclamation points. Fleming took this particular suggestion so much to heart that, in his own words, "I put in exclamation marks like pepper. And my publishers stupidly left them in. Then I get a fierce review from *The New York Times* saying not only is Ian Fleming a very inferior writer but he has the girlish trick of putting in exclamation marks all over the place."

Still, with all his care, he still made factual mistakes, and he learned too late that Vent Vert is made by Balmain and not by Dior, that the Orient Express has vacuum, and not hydraulic, brakes, and that you have mousseline sauce, not béarnaise, with asparagus.

Fleming had certain other habits as a writer that might

be noted here. He kept a notebook which he called his "book of golden words," and when a Daily Express reporter called on him in February, 1964, he copied a few entries from it. There was a notation of the name "Mr. Szasz," which Fleming thought would be ideal for a villain. He had somehow come across the Bulgar proverb "My enemy's enemy is my friend," and if he had lived, it would probably have turned up on the lips of some inscrutable villain. Also in the book was the sentence, "You won't have a lover if you don't love," which was pure Fleming and might have issued as wisdom from some future heroine.

Of course, the most famous example of this trick was the name James Bond itself. At the time he was contemplating *Casino Royale,* he was poking through a book called *Birds of the West Indies,* by a certain James Bond, a well-known ornithologist. Fleming, looking for a name for his hero, whom he conceived of as a blunt instrument, wanted something "suitably flat and colorless." He didn't want a hero along Bulldog Drummond lines but rather someone anonymous whom the action of the book would carry along. When he saw the name James Bond, he thought, "My God, that's the dullest name I've ever heard," and promptly appropriated it. The name later became so associated with adventure and excitement that the wife of the real James Bond (the ornithologist) wrote him a letter thanking him for using it.

After the Bond books had achieved their really big success, Fleming stopped working for the Thomson chain, except for an occasional article, and worked what he called the "Fleming Two-Day Week." This meant that he spent four days and five nights in the country, in a small but comfortable flat on Pegwell Bay, in Sandwich, and two nights in London.

In the country he got up "late"—half past eight or nine —and then had breakfast, consisting of a three-and-a-half minute egg and coffee. He read the papers, fooled with the mail, and then headed for the golf course. He played the Royal St. George, and after lunch there with friends, he went out and played what he termed "a tough game of golf for fairly high stakes." He generally played an unusual game, called Scotch foursomes, where each player hits the ball alternately. Then he returned home to several bourbons and water, dinner and bed.

In London he followed somewhat the same routine, except that the time allotted in the country to golf was spent in a small office in the Temple answering mail with the assistance of a secretary, going over proofs of his latest literary endeavors, and administering the interests of what had by this time become a very big business. In town he ate lunch with male friends; he didn't like lunching with women. After lunch, he sometimes spent an hour or so at one of his clubs, Boodles or the Turf, reading "in that highly civilized privacy which is the great thing about some English clubs."

After an afternoon in the office, he returned home to three stiff drinks and then dinner with friends either at home or outside.

Ian Fleming was often called on to express himself on the subject of suspense fiction, a subject on which he had highly developed and fairly consistent views. Even before he was known as the author of the Bond books, he wrote a short summation of the New York literary scene circa 1950 for *The Sunday Times*, whose title, "Bang-Bang, Kiss-

Kiss," he and other people often used to characterize his own work.

He did not think highly of Mickey Spillane, for he wrote, "I fortified myself for the stratocruiser flight home with 'My Gun Is Quick,' by Mickey Spillane. . . . Alas, on leaving Gander, I found that 'The moonlight on the white V of the plunging neckline made it hard to concentrate' for Mike Hammer, private eye, of whom the Miami 'Herald' critic says: 'In a long and misspent life immersed in blood, I don't believe I have ever met a tougher hombre.' For my money, they come tougher in 'Teddy Lester's Chums.' "

On the other hand, Fleming always professed sincere admiration for the masters of the American tough school, and in the same roundup he wrote: "The homespun American folktales of Raymond Chandler, John O'Hara, James M. Cain, 'Little Caesar' Burnett and others have many admirers." "If the day comes when the harsh voice of the .38 Police Positive is stilled and the office bottle has yielded its last pint of rye," Fleming said, he would no longer be buying many American books.

He once wrote that he wanted to write what he termed "thrillers designed to be read as literature," and listed as other practitioners of this genre Edgar Allan Poe, Dashiell Hammett, Raymond Chandler, Eric Ambler and Graham Greene. He told one interviewer that James Bond was a "believable" hero, after the pattern of Raymond Chandler's and Dashiell Hammett's heroes. On another occasion, when asked to mention writers who had influenced him, he replied, "Two splendid American writers, the great masters of the modern thriller, Dashiell Hammett and Raymond Chandler. I was influenced by these writers, by their extremely good style and the breadth and ingeniousness of their stories. I suppose, if I were to examine the problem in depth, I'd go back to my childhood and find some roots of interest in E. Phillips Oppenheim and Sax Rohmer."

He also admired Simenon, whom he once told, "I read your first books in 1939 on my way to Moscow. I stopped in either Amsterdam or The Hague and there on the book-stall was a whole collection of those very good jackets. . . . I bought three or four to take to Moscow, and I absolutely adored them."

In his statements on suspense fiction, Fleming insisted over and over again on one quality above all others, and that was that the reader must be unable to stop reading. Describing this quality in a review done for *The Spectator* in 1955, Fleming said that for him the masters of suspense "make the pulses of all of us beat faster," and that they do this because "their heroes are credible and their villains terrify with a real 'blackness.' Their situations are fraught with doom, and, above all, they have pace. When one chapter is done, we reach out for the next. Each chapter is a wave to be jumped as we race with exhilaration behind the hero like a water-skier behind a fast motor boat."

Many writers, Fleming believed, did not achieve this pace. It could be defeated by mannered prose, trying for striking verbal effects instead of getting on with the story, or by long descriptions which were not strictly relevant to the narrative. Complicated relationships which the reader would continually have to remind himself about, unusual names, as in Russian novels, so that the reader could not keep the characters identified, or journeys in which the author introduced involved geographies—all of these were, for Fleming, qualities that defeated pace in the suspense novel.

In his 1955 *Spectator* review, Fleming wrote: "The reader is quite happy to share the pillow-fantasies of the author so long as he is provided with sufficient landmarks to help him relate the author's world more or less to his own, and a straining after verisimilitude with maps and diagrams should be avoided except in detective stories aimed at the off-beat mind."

An even worse sin, for Fleming, were recapitulations of the preceding action, in which the hero either thinks over everything that has happened to him in the last twenty-four hours or lines up all the suspects and clues and ponders them. This was anathema to Fleming, who wrote: "When the author drags his feet with this space-filling device he is sacrificing momentum which it will take him much brisk writing to recapture."

Fleming, however, realized that his own work went into a good many details that were not strictly necessary for the action of the book. He wrote: "I confess that I often sin grievously in this respect. I am excited by the poetry of things and places, and the pace of my stories sometimes suffers while I take the reader by the throat and stuff him with great gobbets of what I consider *should* interest him, at the same time shaking him furiously and shouting 'Like this, damn you!' about something that has caught my particular fancy."

At the same time, Fleming believed in grounding his fantasies on a hard rock of closely observed minutiae. He was an observant person himself and remembered things very accurately. He was interested in certain subjects, and these interests are often reflected in his books. He also believed that a good ingredient for his novels was "anything that will thrill the human senses—absolutely anything."

Fleming said that when he came to write his first book, he realized that the plot was fantastic and wondered "how I could anchor it to the ground so it wouldn't take off completely." The answer, he felt, was in piling up concrete details in the incidental parts of the structure, so that the reader would more easily go along with the central absurdity. He believed in using exact names for objects, and the greater the precision of detail, the better. Therefore, cigarette lighters in the Bond books have brand names, Bond's car is a 4½-liter Bentley with an Amherst-Villiers supercharger, the girls use well-known perfumes, and the drinks are prepared to exacting formulas.

Further than this, though, Fleming, himself, was excited by certain kinds of sensory stimuli and felt that it would help his books if he tried to convey this excitement to his readers. He said that in his books the sun was always shining, the food was always good, and the background of the plot was set in interesting and exciting places; that "in general a strong hedonistic streak is always there to offset the grimmer side of James Bond's adventures." He felt that he provided an entirely legitimate kind of escape from a reality that might be drab compared to the somewhat more vivid world which James Bond moved in.

This was not all technique and deception on Fleming's part. He wrote, "While all this sounds devilish crafty, in fact I write about what pleases and stimulates *me,* and if there is a strong streak of hedonism in my books it is there not by guile but because it comes out through the tip of my ball-point pen."

On another occasion he said, "It amuses me to use my powers of observation in my books and at the same time to tell people what my favorite objects are, and my favorite foods and liquors and scents, and so on. Exact details of individual private lives and private tastes are extremely interesting to me. . . . The more we have of this kind of detailed stuff laid down around a character, the more interested we are in him."

Fleming believed in having his hero eat and drink well, though he insisted that he was not, himself, "a card-carrying gourmet." He believed that this was largely a matter of "writing interesting words rather than dull ones." He proposed a hypothetical case in which the choice was between having the hero order the *plat du jour* or a meal of four fried eggs, toast and black coffee because he did not like *plat du jours*. He said there was no snobbism involved here, since the meals would cost about the same and the reason the fried eggs were the better choice was that most people preferred breakfast foods to those served at lunch or dinner, that the hero's ordering the eggs instead of the *plat* proved he was an independent and decisive character, and that the four fried eggs followed by the large black cup of coffee had a decidedly masculine ring to it and was stimulating to the taste buds.

Critics might carp, Fleming added, that this was all nonsense, and he admitted that it would be if reading and writing thrillers were strictly an intellectual occupation, but it wasn't. Banality, he claimed, was the enemy of the thriller writer, and anything that contributed to a "certain disciplined exoticism" was worth undertaking in order to banish any trace of dullness from the thriller.

Fleming, himself, had rather simple tastes in food and drink. He claimed that he would "eat or drink almost anything so long as it tastes good." He wrote an article for *Holiday*, "London's Best Dining," in which he said, "I think good English food is the best in the world. The food I like eating in London and which I regard as unsurpassed is: Colchester and Whitstable oysters; all English fish, particularly Dover soles; Scottish smoked salmon; potted shrimps; lamb cutlets; roast beef; York ham; nearly all the English vegetables, particularly asparagus and peas; English savouries and most English fruits."

He liked American martinis, as did his hero, but admitted they were somewhat hard to find in London. He wrote: "It is extremely difficult to get a good Martini anywhere in England. . . . The way I get one to suit me in any pub is to walk calmly and confidently up to the bar and, speaking very distinctly, ask the man or girl behind it to put plenty of ice in the shaker (they nearly all have a shaker), pour in six gins and one dry vermouth (enunciate 'dry' carefully) and shake until I tell them to stop.

"You then point to a suitably large glass and ask them to pour the mixture in. Your behaviour will create a certain amount of astonishment, not unmixed with fear, but you will have achieved a very large and fairly good Martini, and it will cost you about $1.25."

He liked Norwegian honey for breakfast, and one of his favorite restaurants was Scott's at Piccadilly Circus, where he often lunched, after a martini, on oysters followed by a Scotch woodcock (scrambled eggs topped with anchovies).

He thought that "stout, notably Guinness, is an excellent drink with oysters and fish. Even better is Black Velvet, which is half-and-half stout and champagne in a tankard."

On a tough winter day he liked steak, kidney, and oyster pudding, and he was also fond of filets of sole or plaice, either broiled or meunière. He was not interested in desserts or cheese and, since he was quite a heavy smoker, did not put away large quantities of any kind of food. He was interested in clarets and champagne but was more apt to drink martinis, brandy and ginger ale, or bourbon and branch if left to his own devices.

James Bond shared his interest in automobiles with his creator. Fleming gave him his supercharged Bentley because he liked Bond to use "dashing, interesting things," but also because he would have liked to have owned one himself and also because Amherst Villiers was a friend of his.

Fleming never drove a Bentley himself and said that he couldn't be bothered babying cars that were highly tuned or that wouldn't start in the morning after being left out in the street at night. Nevertheless, he liked a sporty looking vehicle and confessed that "the chorus of 'Smashing!' 'Cor!' and 'Rraauu!' " which he received as he whizzed along in his Thunderbird was "the perfume of Araby."

Before switching to the Thunderbird, Fleming had owned a long string of British vehicles. After a khaki Standard, he had a khaki Morris Oxford, which was demolished by a "gravity-propelled trolley laden with cement blocks" which hit the Morris broadside and knocked both it and Fleming off a small bridge into an adjacent stream.

He then bought a sporty looking 16/80 open Lagonda after falling in love with "the whine of its gears and its outside brake," but gave it up when he found it would barely do seventy and changed to a supercharged Graham Paige convertible coupe, which he donated to the ambulance service at the start of World War II.

During the war he owned an Opel. This came to grief: "One night at the height of the blitz I was dining with Sefton Delmer in his top-floor flat in Lincoln's Inn. A direct hit blew out the lower three floors and left us swilling champagne and waiting for the top floor to fall into the chasm. The fireman who finally hauled us out and down his ladder was so indignant at our tipsy insouciance that I made him a present of the crumpled remains of the Opel."

After the war he owned a Renault and a Hillman Minx before buying a 2½-liter Riley, which developed expensive troubles after running well for over a year. He then had a Sapphire, which he called "a fast, comfortable car, but one which made me feel too elderly when it was going slowly and too nervous when it was going fast."

He then picked up a Daimler, but said he couldn't stand the "ugliness of the rump" and the fact that the engine ran so cool that the heater wouldn't work in winter. A friend said he dropped the Daimler for another reason: Fleming's wife remarked that he looked like the late Queen Mary when he was behind the wheel.

After this he was in the big money and decided to buy himself a really luxurious car. He thought of a Lancia Gran Turismo but decided it was "like driving an angry washing machine" and that at over three thousand pounds it was just a little too much. Then he saw a Thunderbird in the street "and fell head over heels in love."

Still, he hesitated before he bought, and considered a Mercedes. He particularly liked the SL model, but considered it a disadvantage that it "only has room beside the driver for a diminutive blonde with a sponge bag. Moreover, when you open those bat-like doors in the rain, the rain pours straight into the car."

Fleming finally dug down for the three thousand pounds for the T-Bird and was rewarded (so he claimed) with an indignant wife who said that the car was hideous and that there was no room to take people to the station in it. (This was the early two-seater Thunderbird.) Fleming liked not taking people to the station and hung on to the car, despite his wife's further protestations about "a new disease called 'Thunderbird neck' which" he reported, "she complains she gets in the passenger seat."

At the time he wrote his *Spectator* article in 1958 (from which some of the above is quoted), Fleming had owned a Thunderbird for over two years and gone 27,000 miles without any substantial mechanical difficulties, and he had high praise for this car. He wrote: "The reason why I particularly like the Thunderbird, apart from the beauty of its line and the drama of its snarling mouth and the giant, flaring nostril of its air-intake, is that everything works. Absolutely nothing goes wrong."

He admitted that the Thunderbird was not a precision instrument like its English counterparts, but liked this because it allowed for a wider margin of error in the working parts. He liked the hardtop in winter and the soft top in summer, the heater that heated, the wipers that wiped, and the engine that never overheated and started in the morning. The engine and everything about the car had a solid feel for

him. He could do over a hundred and still feel that he had
another twenty m.p.h. in reserve, and at that speed the
brakes held without danger.

Fleming, in fact, was a walking advertisement for the
better American cars. He felt that they were more consistent
and reliable than anything the English produced at a com-
parable price. Since Fleming is sometimes accused of snob-
bishness and anti-Americanism, it is interesting to see that
he enthusiastically opted for the better artifacts of modern
American mass production. (He also considered American
vermouth superior to continental varieties.)

When he eventually switched from a Thunderbird, after
owning the later four-seater, which he considered "less
good," Fleming moved to Studebaker's Avanti. When an
English newspaper asked a number of prominent people to
pick their ideal cars, Fleming replied:

I would choose a Studebaker Avanti, full four-seater, V-8
Gran Sport supercharged by Paxton, styled by Raymond Loewy.
Price around £ 3000.

Having driven two Thunderbirds for six years, during which
not a light bulb has fused and paint and chromium have not
wilted, despite a garageless life, I have become wedded to American cars when they have something approximating European
styling.

I am now switching to the Studebaker, which has always produced first-class cars and which has now with the Avanti created
something really startling—top speed with four up of over 160
m.p.h. and acceleration of 0-60 in 7.4 seconds. My model,
packed with intelligent gimmicks such as switches in the roof,
aircraft type levers for the heating, disc brakes and powerful
built-in roll bar in case I turn over, is being delivered in a few
weeks.

When he got the car, he was delighted with it and found it possessed the same durability and reliability as the Thunderbird plus "much better, tighter road holding and steering than the Thunderbird."

So Fleming shared with Bond an abiding passion for automobiles. He concluded his article for the *Spectator* by writing: "Cyril Connolly once said to me that, if men were honest, they would admit that their motorcars came next after their women and children in their list of loves. I won't go all the way with him on that, but I do enjoy well-designed and attractively wrapped bits of machinery that really work."

Fleming also became interested in the expertise of guns through an exchange of letters with the celebrated gun expert Geoffrey Boothroyd on the proper armament for Bond. Although Fleming had been on the Sandhurst shooting team and had a somewhat more than casual acquaintance with the subject because of this and his experience in Naval Intelligence, he did not consider himself an expert. In fact, after writing of his exchange of letters with Boothroyd for *Sports Illustrated,* he received a number of letters on the subject which he immediately passed on to Boothroyd because he did not consider himself competent to comment on the questions they asked.

Boothroyd originally wrote Fleming commenting on Bond's use of a .25 Beretta. This Boothroyd considered "a lady's gun, and not a really nice lady at that." He advised arming Bond with a revolver and thought the best bet for him might be an S & W .38 Centennial Airweight, because he would then "have a real man-stopper weighing only 17 ounces loaded." The advantage of the larger calibers, Boothroyd told Fleming in a further letter, is "that when you hit someone with a man-stopping bullet they are out of the game and won't lie on the floor still popping at you."

Fleming became intrigued by both Boothroyd and these suggestions and eventually went into a number of other matters with him, such as the right kind of holster for a really fast draw—Boothroyd recommended a "Lightning" Berns-Martin Triple Draw Holster instead of the chamois-leather pouch which Bond favored at that time. The chamois leather, Boothroyd said, would be "ideal for *carrying* a gun, but God help him if he has to get it out in a hurry. The soft leather will snag and foul on the projecting parts of the gun and he will still be struggling to get the gun out when the other fellow is counting the holes in Bond's tummy."

When Fleming asked Boothroyd for advice on silencers for Bond's weapons, Boothroyd replied: "With apologies, I think you will find that silencers are more often found in fiction than in real life. An effective silencer on an auto pistol would be very ponderous and would spoil the balance of the gun, and to silence a revolver would be even more difficult due to the gas escape between the cylinder and the barrel. Personally I can't at this stage see how one would fit a silencer to a Beretta unless a special barrel were made for it, as the silencer has to be screwed on to the barrel, and as you know there is very little of the barrel projecting in front of the slide on the Beretta."

Fleming also asked Boothroyd for advice on what Bond's enemies in SMERSH might be carrying and received back quite a long list of possibilities, including various types of Lugers, Mausers, Walthers from Germany, a Polish Radom

35, the Russian Tokarev Model 30, and the Japanese Nambu, for, he said, the Russians "do not hesitate to use foreign weapons if they are better than those produced by themselves."

Fleming's correspondence with Boothroyd led to an amusing incident. For the cover of the Johnathan Cape (his English publishers) edition of *From Russia, with Love*, Fleming wanted a *trompe l'oeil* painting of a gun crossed with a rose and borrowed Boothroyd's own S & W .38 Special M & P for the artist to use as a model for the revolver. No sooner was the gun in the artist's hands than a multiple murder took place in Glasgow of three people—wife, daughter and sister-in-law—and the bullets proved to be .38 caliber. Police records showed that Boothroyd owned a .38 and they stepped around and asked him about it, whereupon he referred them to a certain Ian Fleming in London.

A few hours later the CID were closeted with Fleming, who fortunately could produce an alibi for the night of the murder as well as a firearms certificate from his Naval Intelligence days, but could not produce the weapon in question, which he had already passed on to the artist, Richard Chopping.

Fleming pleaded with the CID not to go out on a manhunt for Chopping, and after he had shown the sergeant his complete correspondence with Boothroyd and the CID had made voluminous notes, they agreed to leave Chopping alone provided the .38 were quickly placed in their hands. The incident came to a happy conclusion when Chopping showed up the next day with the cover painting and Fleming gave the revolver to the CID. The cover turned out to be a tremendous success, and Chopping designed all the remaining covers for the Bond books.

The upshot of all this expertise was that in *Doctor No,* Fleming introduced the figure of the Armourer, a certain "Major Boothroyd," who persuaded Bond to change holsters and guns. However, Fleming had become entangled in all the expertise and gave Bond an S & W .38 Centennial Airweight for long-range work, although the real Boothroyd had suggested this as a close-up gun, and put a Walther PPK 7.65-mm. into the Berns-Martin holster, whereupon the real Boothroyd received a letter from another expert who stated: "If he [Bond] carries on using this PPK out of that Berns-Martin rig I shall have to break down and write a rude letter to Fleming. I realize that writers have a whole lot of license but this is going too far!"

All of this shows the extent Fleming would go to in order to get something right in his books, but it also shows that expertise like this is really a private game the author plays with himself. The only thing that counts to most readers, who wouldn't know a Walther PPK from a Red Ryder BB gun, is that the whole business sound right, and the fact that a Beretta was not a very effective pistol for close combat did not bother them in the least. For Fleming, however, merely becoming involved in the whole subject probably made all his subsequent reference to guns (right or wrong) more interesting, because he was more interested in the subject than he had previously been. And that, for him—writing more interesting words and more interesting books— was the real justification of all this kind of thing.

An even more important ingredient than expertise for the successful thriller was the hero of that thriller, and here again Fleming had strong, consistent opinions. We have already seen that he admired Hammett and Chandler and he thought of James Bond as being in the tradition of their heroes, Philip Marlowe and Sam Spade. He said Bond was "a sort of amalgam of romantic tough guys, dressed up in 20th Century clothes, using 20th Century language," and he believed he was closer to the real agents he had known in Naval Intelligence than to "any of the rather cardboardy heroes of the ancient thrillers."

Still, Fleming knew that Bond was "highly romanticized." He was often asked whether he were Bond, and he always said that aside from liking certain of the same kinds of liquor and cigarettes, there was little similarity between them. In the areas of sex and violence, this was certainly true. Fleming actually disliked violence of any kind and strongly objected when private detectives of Anthony Eden killed a number of giant bush rats outside Fleming's Jamaican residence when Eden was using it to recuperate after an operation. Still, friends observed that Fleming was "awfully like Bond really, appearance, clothes, Floris bath essence and all."

Fleming sometimes explained the real relationship between James Bond and his creator in another way. "It's very much the Walter Mitty syndrome," he said, "the author's feverish dreams of what he might have been—bang bang, kiss kiss. . . . It's what you would expect of an adolescent mind, which I happen to possess."

Another close friend defined it in another way. "Ian," he said, "is very fundamentally a hero-worshipper. He loves physical achievement in the face of adversity. It began in his awe of his older brother, Peter, who had explored the

Brazilian jungles, crossed the roof of China, and written fine books about his experiences. He worships Sugar Ray Robinson and Jacques Cousteau, the skin diver."

Fleming himself once accounted for Bond's popularity in the need we all have for heroes. He said: "I think the reason for his success is that people are lacking in heroes in real life today. Heroes are always getting knocked— Philip and Mountbatten are examples of this—and I think people absolutely long for heroes. The thing that's wrong with the new anticolonialism is that no one has yet found a Negro hero. . . . Well, I don't regard James Bond precisely as a hero, but at least he does get on and do his duty, in an extremely corny way, and in the end, after giant despair, he wins the girl or the jackpot or whatever it may be."

Fleming never took an overly serious view of his own work, although as much of the above would indicate, he believed in doing whatever he did as well as he possibly could. He said, "I write unashamedly for pleasure and money." He also wrote:

I am not an angry young or even middle-aged man. I am not "involved." My books are not "engaged."

I have no message for suffering humanity and . . . I have never been tempted to foist . . . harrowing personal experiences on the public.

My opuscula do not aim at changing people or making them go out and do something.

They are not designed to find favour with the Homintern. They are written for warm-blooded heterosexuals in railway trains, airplanes or beds.

In a joint interview with Simenon, Fleming remarked that he had no greater literary ambitions. "I've no ambitions at all to write a novel," he said. "When I've finished writing James Bond I don't think I shall write any more."

When Ken Purdy asked him about this, he said that he thought he succeeded in communicating enjoyment and this was a pretty good achievement. This was in line with his often stated view that he had "fun" writing the books and that if they were at all successful, it was because they communicated this quality to the reader. He said in another interview, "I think it's an absolute miracle that an elderly person like me can go on turning out these books with such zest. It's really a terrible indictment of my own character— they're so adolescent. But they're fun. I think people like them because they're fun."

Yet he also told Purdy that he thought he wrote somewhat below his "ultimate capacity," and that if he really sat down and tried hard enough he might be able to write the *War and Peace* of modern thrillers. Still, he thought that someone like Graham Greene or Simenon would be more likely to bring it off because "I'm more interested in action than in cerebration," and also because "I enjoyed exaggeration and things larger than life. It amuses me to have a villain with a great bulbous head, whereas, as you know, they're generally little people with nothing at all extraordinary about them."

He also suspected that he worked too fast and didn't have the patience to write a book with sufficient depth for this classic thriller. But this didn't really bother him: "I must say, I'm very happy writing as I do. And I greatly enjoy knowing that other people, quite intelligent people, find my books amusing and entertaining. But I'm not really surprised, because they entertain and amuse me too."

Critics didn't worry Fleming greatly. Al Hart, his first American editor at Macmillan and Company, said he was genuinely amused by parodies of his work, and particularly valued one that appeared in *Punch* early in his career. He thought it was his first real recognition.

In an interview he said, "Actually, I'm as interested in my bad reviews as I am in my good ones, because very often they deal with a legitimate complaint. I regard my *oeuvres* in a very humble fashion, so I really don't mind if somebody gives me a kick in the pants. I think I deserve it anyway."

Some of the more blatantly high-minded of his detractors did get under his skin. When Ken Purdy asked him about the charge that he was "obsessed" with violence, he replied that ours is a violent age and like all popular heroes Bond reflected his own time. Fleming also said that the tortures Bond underwent were derived from those practiced on real secret agents, and that the real thing was often considerably worse than anything he described. He said he had never received this criticism from men who knew the subject as he did.

As for Bond's sexual habits, Fleming said, "Perhaps Bond's blatant heterosexuality is a subconscious protest against the current fashion for sexual confusion."

He thought his harsher critics had "so many chips on their shoulders they should go into the timber business." And his final comment on the subject was: "I am not an entrant in the Shakespeare stakes."

In all the current hurrah for Fleming and Bond, it is sometimes difficult to recall from what relatively modest beginnings this giant oak has grown. The first Bond books were barely reviewed, and except in Fleming's own *Sunday Times,* the reviews were scarcely raves. In the United States, in particular, the fad took a long time growing and none of his early novels sold more than ten thousand copies in their hardcover editions. Anthony Boucher of *The New York Times,* who is the big critical gun in the suspense and mystery field, didn't like the Bond books and said so frequently.

Still, by 1958 something had started to happen. Despite two memorable blasts in the British high-brow press (or perhaps because of them), Fleming had by this point accumulated an estimated 1,250,000 readers. He had had several good notices to offset the others, one from his friend Raymond Chandler, who called him "masterly," and another from novelist Elizabeth Bowen, who said, "Here's magnificent writing."

Although the English market was very strong for Bonds in the late fifties, the American lagged far behind. By 1961 Fleming was with his second American publisher, Viking Press, which had followed Macmillan. Neither they nor American Library, which had bought paperback rights from the two U. S. hardcover publishers, had done very well with Bond, though all had been encouraged by the English success and thought that the books might get rolling over here. Then Fleming had the benefit of some wonderful publicity which made his fortune for him.

Fleming already knew that President Kennedy enjoyed his books. He told *The New Yorker*: "A couple of years ago, when I was in Washington, and was driving to lunch with a friend of mine, Margaret Leiter, she spotted a young couple coming out of church and she stopped our cab. 'You must meet them,' she said. 'They're great fans of yours.'

And she introduced me to Jack and Jackie Kennedy. 'Not *the* Ian Fleming!' they said. What could be more gratifying than that? They asked me to dinner that night, with Joe Alsop and some other characters. I think the President likes my books because he enjoys the combination of physical violence, effort, and winning in the end—like his PT-boat experiences. I think James Bond may be good for him after the dry pack of the day."

The press got hold of this information and the effect on Fleming's sales was staggering. Jay Tower, the publicity director of New American Library, said:

He wasn't doing very well in this country up to then. We couldn't understand it. He had all the ingredients. We thought he should sell very well to American readers of suspense.

We decided to really push the books. We had a sales conference and planned new covers of all the Fleming books. We scheduled a January teaser campaign. But we weren't sure any of this would work. A few weeks later we had fabulous good fortune. President Kennedy said he loved Fleming.

Then Fleming made Jackie Kennedy's list of books. When Bobby Kennedy came along and got on the bandwagon the ball was rolling pretty fast. Everybody under the sun wanted a Fleming book.

The next step in the great success saga was the movies, the first of which, *Doctor No,* appeared in 1962. Though not quite the same thing as the books, which they took with a considerable grain of salt, audiences liked them from the first. Script writer Richard Maibaum wrote: "The common denominator is deadpan spoofing. We know it, the audience know it, yet they are perfectly willing to alternately believe and disbelieve what is happening on the screen."

Fleming seemed to be of two minds about the films. Of course, he was ecstatic about the money they brought (he always insisted that he wrote primarily for money), but like all writers he did feel a bit troubled about any tampering with his material. He protested the deletion of the famous crabs in the original script of *Doctor No* and said of the finished product, "Those who've read the book are likely to be disappointed, but those who haven't will find it a wonderful movie. Audiences laugh in all the right places."

The films brought Fleming even greater popularity, and he was so constantly photographed and mentioned that he finally began to achieve the ultimate—instant recognition by the man in the street. Phyllis Jackson, his New York agent, said, "He gets an enormous kick out of being recognized. We had movie stars in the office all the time and the secretaries never looked up from their typewriters. But when Fleming walked in, and they were told who he was they flocked around him. I think maybe it's because his hero is bigger than life."

Another New York acquaintance said that Fleming really didn't care for the excessive adulation his new-won fame sometimes exposed him to, but that he genuinely enjoyed success and wanted it. By 1964 this success had reached large enough proportions for Fleming to take the highly unusual step of selling a majority interest in himself to a London-based sugar, rum and insurance empire, Booker Brothers, McConnell and Company.

Fleming himself had already incorporated himself as Glidrose Productions, Limited, a not unusual step for successful people whose main asset is their talents. This and the later sale were, of course, mainly tax saving devices. "I seem to make a lot of money," Fleming said, "but in the end I have about as much as a judge or a Cabinet minister to spend—five or six thousand pounds."

Great Britain's tax system taxed incomes heavily, but when Fleming sold 51 per cent of himself, there was no capital gains tax, and so the 280,000 dollars he realized on the deal was his to keep. The Booker Brothers contract did not include movie, television or other subsidiary rights, and Fleming felt that the 49 per cent of himself that he held on to would provide enough of a carrot to keep him working. "I still have an incentive to work," he said, "since I still get that much of the total book income."

By the summer of 1964, Ian Fleming's books had sold an estimated 21,000,000 English language copies. This included 14,500,000 United States paperbacks and 250,000 American hardcover books, plus another 6,500,000 hard- and soft-cover books in England. *The New York Times* estimated that his books alone had earned him $2,800,000. When he died his estate was valued at £ 289,170, on which a duty of £ 210,366 had already been paid.

After his death, the Bond success went on at an even greater rate. The three films already made continued to make tremendous grosses. When a double bill of *Doctor No* and *From Russia, with Love* was revived recently, it did almost as well the second time around as it had the first. By the time all three current attractions have had their run, they will probably have grossed over a hundred million dollars.

And the movies were not hurting the sale of the books— far from it. New American Library recently brought out the paperback edition of *You Only Live Twice* in a first printing of 2,700,000 copies, which the publisher believes to be the largest first printing in history. The publisher announced at the same time that it had a total of 30,000,000 Bond books in print.

Meanwhile, other products, which Fleming had done his best to discourage when he was alive, proliferated. In France six thousand stores sold three million dollars' worth of Bond merchandise in February and March of 1965, including a thirty-dollar black-leather attaché case, an eighty-dollar trench coat with a silk lining garnished with 007's, and a five-dollar set of 007 cuff links. Australia contributed an 007 snorkel, a Bond handkerchief, and a Bond tuxedo to the boom. For the ladies there were 007 chocolates and unmentionables, plugged by the slogan, "Become fit for James Bond."

In the United States, Colgate-Palmolive rushed out a line of 007 toilet goods, and there were 007 raincoats by Spatz and a "James Bond Secret Agent 007 Game." The licensing agents did not think they were engaged in any quickie promotion. One of them, Jay Emmett, of the Licensing Corporation of America, said: "In today's world there are lots of people who think James Bond really existed. They even feel he is still operating somewhere—I always used to believe in Sherlock Holmes. That's why this isn't just one of those movie promotions. It will go on forever."

The complicated tax arrangements Ian Fleming made toward the end of his life were prompted by a feeling that he had to do something to protect his own family. He had had one heart attack in 1961, and although the doctors told him, as they always do, to slow down, Fleming had a tough time obeying orders. He cut his cigarettes from sixty a day to thirty, but that was about the extent of his slowing down.

A friend in New York said, "He always drove himself. He lived hard and played hard and he was unwilling to live on any other terms."

By the end of his life, Fleming had most of the things he wanted—enough money to enjoy life, a family, and the kind of work he liked doing. He seemed a happy man. He told an interviewer:

One can only be grateful for the talent that came out of the air, and to one's capacity for hard, concentrated effort. I am perhaps the smallest and most profitable one-man factory in the world.

If I chose to leave England and live somewhere like Switzerland I could be a millionaire.

I don't want yachts, racehorses or a Rolls-Royce. I want my family and my friends and good health and to have a small treadmill with a temperature of 80° in the shade and the sea to come to every year for two months.

And to be able to work there and look at the flowers and birds and fish, and somehow to give pleasure to people in the millions. Well, you can't ask for more.

In August, 1964, Fleming suffered his second heart attack at Sandwich. He told the hospital attendants who came to pick him up, "I'm sorry to have troubled you chaps." He died a few hours later.

Many of his friends feel that the simple epitaph which he wrote for James Bond in *You Only Live Twice* was also meant as his own. It read: "I shall not waste my days in trying to prolong them. I shall use my time."

CHAPTER

5

The World of James Bond

THE immense success of the Bond novels leads to a persistent question: Why are they popular? We have seen that Fleming, himself, was somewhat impatient with riddles of this kind, saying that since they were fun to write they were presumably fun to read. This kind of question-begging is all very well for the author of our pleasures, but the questions persist.

After all, a great many things are fun, yet some of us choose certain pleasures over others. More pertinently, one object may appear on the surface to be very similar to another object, yet one gives us pleasure and the other does not. The bookstores and magazine racks are these days more than ever filled with books that have many of the qualities of the Bond novels. Yet none of these books has attained anything like their success. If one has only the most ordinary kind of curiosity, he is bound to wonder about such a state of affairs.

Moreover, there is a school of thought which tells us that we can take the measure of our society by examining those objects and activities which are most in vogue. The idea here is that any tune to which a great many of us dance discloses some fundamental twitch in our social condition to which we are responding. The student of these matters can, by close attention to the tune, learn a good deal about the dancers.

There are perils to this line of thinking. In the first place, it is often difficult to uncover the fundamental quality which is leading the population to such rites of universal idolatry, and what is one man's *Zeitgeist* is often for the next observer a trivial and transitory fad. Even more common is the failure to notice that for any popular phenomenon pointing to one trend in contemporary society, there is often an equally popular artifact pointing in the exactly opposite direction.

It is perhaps this habit of drawing sweeping conclusions from limited data that gave Fleming cause to doubt some of the interpretations which were placed on his work. The most famous of these, an article by English critic Paul Johnson in the *New Statesman* called "Sex, Snobbery, and Sadism," was a massive condemnation of Bond and anyone who had ever read him with even mild pleasure.

This article started by saying, "I have just finished what is, without doubt, the nastiest book I have ever read," and then went on to catalogue, in detail, what Mr. Johnson considered its nastiness. The book was *Dr. No,* and Mr. Johnson claims he would have stopped reading it a third of the way through if he had not realized he was on to "a social phenomenon of some importance."

Johnson pontificated that Fleming "deliberately and systematically excites, and then satisfies the worst instincts of his readers." The reason for the popularity of the books, Johnson stated, was "our curious post-war society, with its obsessive interest in debutantes, its cult of U and non-U, its working class graduates educated into snobbery by the welfare state . . . a soft market for Mr. Fleming's poison."

This was not the worst of the matter for Mr. Johnson, who concluded: "Recently, I read Henri Alleg's horrifying account of his tortures in an Algiers prison; and I have on my desk a documented study of how we treat our prisoners in Cyprus. I am no longer astonished that these things can happen. Indeed, after reflecting on the Fleming phenomenon, they seem to me almost inevitable."

Now all this, and there is more of it in Mr. Johnson's sermon, is the worst kind of social-critical bombast. To take the most obvious point, our post-war society with its interest in debutantes and the novels of Ian Fleming does not need to figure in any discussion of the brutal treatment of prisoners under conditions of guerrilla warfare. The Redcoats who executed Yankee irregulars in South Carolina during the American Revolution had not read Ian Fleming, and the conflicting forces in Vietnam, who are not at all kind towards one another, have no knowledge nor interest in debutantes.

But perhaps this is scoring too easily off Mr. Johnson, a patently high-minded individual, who is often dismayed by the low-minded mortals he finds all around him. One basic difficulty with this kind of criticism of popular works dealing with frequent acts of violence, is that the critics are apt to forget that popular literature has always dealt with such subjects and probably always will. If one must play the psychologist, it is fairly safe to argue that men are not always peaceful creatures. During the course of their lives they undergo a great many unpleasant experiences to which they would dearly like to respond with a shot in the mouth aimed at the nearest human target, but they are often prevented from doing so by the usages of polite society and the policeman on the beat. Nevertheless, the urge is there and it is quite a powerful urge, and if you cannot do it yourself, the next best thing is to read about it or watch it on television. All this is quite ignoble, of course, but it exists and it is certainly nothing new.

Sex is also a fairly popular subject with the masses and doubtless will remain so. The only way for Mr. Johnson and others of a similar turn of mind to make a valid point would be to show that Fleming's novels are somehow unique in either the quantity or quality of the sex and violence. I suspect, however, that they are ill-equipped to make such a point, mainly because they are unfamiliar with what their friends and neighbors have been reading for the past decade or so.

At your favorite drugstore, you can, without trying very hard, find novels of suspense and intrigue that make Mr. Fleming's tales look pale indeed. In all of the Bond novels (with the possible exception of *The Spy Who Loved Me*), sex is certainly an incidental ingredient of the plot. James Bond comes across girls and makes love to them, but his relationship to them is never the dominant concern of the novel.

The point is not that Ian Fleming is as pure as Jane
Austen or Henry James, but that if you are really interested
in sex and violence and have fifty cents to spend, Fleming
does not really satisfy you as well as many other writers
whose works are equally available. And it is not only a
question of quantity. Fleming not only does not supply as
much sex and violence per page as many of his contemporaries, but even when he is doing his damnedest on the
subject, he is neither as provocative as some writers nor as
lovingly detailed as others.

Theories about the popularity of Fleming's work pro-
liferate. John le Carré, the author of *The Spy Who Came In
from the Cold*, had this to say:

> Now this James Bond business, the really interesting thing,
> you know, is that this Bond himself would be what I would
> describe as the ideal defector. Because if the money was better,
> the booze freer, the women easier over there in Moscow, he'd
> be off like a shot and defect to the Russians.
> Bond, you see, is the ultimate prostitute. He replaces love with
> technique. For Bond it isn't a question of why you kill people
> but how; it isn't a question of whether you seduce people but
> when. None of this would matter and Fleming himself is least
> of all to blame, but when they have made an institution of Bond
> they must either make him respectable or destroy him. At the
> moment they seem to be sticking to the first alternative. I think
> Bond may even be a useful social phenomenon; he puts under
> one hat a great number of contemporary maladjustments. We
> need him as a mirror.

Malcolm Muggeridge thought that the Bond books were a
form of contemporary daydream. He said in *The Observer*:
"As a hero of our time, Bond is deplorable enough. One
wishes people had better dreams, but Fleming himself is

scarcely to be blamed. He only gave them a form. I remember discussing his writing with him, when he was at work on *Casino Royale,* his first book. He was insistent that he had no 'literary' aspiration at all, and that his only purpose was to make money and provide entertainment. Here I think he deceived himself. He was deeply serious about the Bond books, and Bond became increasingly a glamourized version of himself. That so essentially kindly and, in the nicest way, 'ordinary' a person should *want* to be Bond is extraordinary enough. It was, I decided, a kind of illness, but one, as it turned out, so widespread as to reach the dimensions of a plague."

Richard Mayne, in the *New Statesman,* thought that the Bond novels were all the rage because they provided "excuses to wallow in the type of reading we dropped at adolescence. From the first," he went on, "Ian Fleming provided excuses, er, galore. There was the expertise on games, the Braine-like attention to branded products, the apparent authenticity of some of the cold war trimmings, the knowing literacy of much of the writing, the hints of self-parody that the films carry almost to the point of farce. For the first time in blood-and-thunder writing, the blood was no longer merely cosmetic, and the sex went beyond either Buchan's or Sapper's, beyond Dornford Yate's winsomeness or Leslie Charteris's use of the implicit. Bond wasn't superhuman; was a civil servant who got really badly beaten up; instead of Raymond Chandler's innocuous great black pool closing over Marlowe's head when the villains mugged him, Bond and Felix Leiter suffered the kind of treatment that their authentic counterparts risk and get."

Finally, *Newsweek* proclaimed in its Fleming obituary:

In a way, for all their arbitrary violence, Fleming's novels and the movies made from them were a series of civilized acts. What won him his vast readership was nothing so simple as mere escapism. Bond is a hero in an age of anti-heroes. Deeply flawed with contemporaneity, snobbish about "fine" things, yet insensitive to beauty, lacking a centered self, tethered to the impersonal State, he nevertheless has the freedom to operate in a realm of modern dragons and demons.

For Bond is not so much the protagonist of a thriller as the agent of a myth. Surrounded by precisely named objects to create a sense of plausibility, he tracks down the psyche's oppressors and slays them. A child of his era, Fleming politicized these oppressors—making them Russian spies or Nazi master criminals. Moreover, as British novelist Kingsley Amis noted, he "technologized" the process of their pursuit and downfall. In this fusion of fact and fancy lies one secret of his appeal both to romantics and to minds as precise as that of President Kennedy.

All these speculations about the Bond mystique may rise out of a vague feeling that Fleming's books lack one basic ingredient which we would expect them to have and which he himself insisted was the most important element of any thriller. The Bond books do not really prompt one to keep turning the pages, and what happens next is not a matter of real concern.

This may seem a startling statement to make about the most widely known "suspense" novels in recent years, yet I think the case can be established. In a classic detective thriller in which suspense is generated, it is done by means of a logical unfolding of an established situation. To take a hypothetical case—three people are alone in a house; one of them is murdered. The novel as it unfolds will gradually uncover the relationships between these people until a point is reached at which we will see, through the accumulation of physical and psychological "clues," that X and not Y had to be the murderer.

In the typical Eric Ambler novel, a man from an ordinary middle-class existence is plunged into the strange intrigue-laden world of Istanbul, which is dangerous to him because of something he has accidentally done. As the plot moves through time, the hero gradually discovers just how devious all the intrigues are and how dangerous they all are to him, until finally, at the point of death, he realizes how truly dark and evil this world really is and does something about it.

Common to these plots, hypothetical and real, is the build-up of suspense through a series of discoveries and sur-prises, *all the elements of which are contained in the situa-tion as it is originally established,* all of which lead logically to the climax. Now, this is precisely what does not happen in any of Fleming's plots. In any Fleming book, gratuitous elements are always added along the way, or in some of the worst cases, the situation itself changes completely, so that we do not come to know all the dynamism that the original material contained. Instead, new ingredients are constantly thrown at us until the time comes for James Bond to triumph and for the villain to be discomfited.

Fleming's first book, *Casino Royale,* is badly conceived in terms of suspense. The problem is that Fleming, after setting up with great care the opposition of Le Chiffre and Bond, has Le Chiffre killed before the novel is over and has to invent a totally new intrigue involving Bond and the girl, Vesper Lynd, who is supposed to be on Bond's side but turns out to be working for the enemy.

Still worse, the contest between Bond and Le Chiffre is not decided by the contestants but by another outside force which is also trying to destroy Le Chiffre and which gets him just in time to save Bond's skin.

The objection to this is that Fleming is really not playing the game when he manages things in this offhand fashion, and that because he does not play the game he botches the suspense he may have created along the way. Fleming's novels have a peculiar structure, considering the genre into which they fall. They are usually a string of episodes concerning two combatants, with a certain amount of suspense built up within each episode but dissipated at the episode's conclusion.

In *Casino Royale* this is particularly obvious because, as I have said, the structure of the whole book seems to fall apart with the death of Le Chiffre. Even considering the Le Chiffre episode as a self-contained narrative, the same pattern prevails. After a short gambling scene and some expertise with M in London, Bond gets to the casino and is introduced to the subsidiary characters, Mathis and Leiter, who will help him.

If one were really trying to pick nits, he could criticize these people as not really necessary to the central confrontation between Bond and Le Chiffre, but on the other hand bringing in these extra agents does make the whole affair seem more important, and this is perhaps a legitimate device. However, it should be noted that, as Fleming himself admitted, he does tend to get interested in subsidiary matters at the expense of the plot.

This is just what happens in *Casino Royale* when, after the bungled bomb-throwing by the Bulgars, Bond takes

Vesper Lynd to dinner before having it out with Le Chiffre over the *chemin-de-fer* table. There is a lot of food plus a lesson in drinkmanship in Chapter Eight, "Pink Lights and Champagne," but the sustained mood of menace which the bomb-throwing creates simply drops out of sight. Now, admitting that Bond's demonstrations of taste are necessary to the world Fleming creates, they certainly do not favor the suspense element. In fact the part of James Bond that seems to live constantly surrounded by luxuries out of advertisements from *The New Yorker* creates an atmosphere of easy living that does not lead to thoughts of sudden, irrefutable death, which the best suspense fiction demands.

It is very different from the atmosphere in which Raymond Chandler's Philip Marlowe moves, where even when the facade is gilded, there is in the eye of the beholder the constant suspicion that all is hollowness and deceit. In Marlowe's Los Angeles, the dusty rooming houses where the idle poor spend their days in joyless carousing are always felt to be part of the same city as the swimming pools, night clubs and mansions of some of Marlowe's clients. Marlowe's world is a whole one, where every stone cries murder. Bond, however, alternates easily between a world in which he is the target of SMERSH bombs, and dinners with carafes of ice-cold vodka and girls in black velvet dresses which they are afraid of crushing—and the two spheres are not joined organically.

Fleming's next book, *Live and Let Die,* is more typical of his work in terms of its plot. While Fleming often uses a few pages at the end to round out his stories, it is very unusual for him to do in the villain as hastily as he did in *Casino Royale*. In *Live and Let Die*, Mr. Big hangs on until the end, and the final clash with Bond is exciting. Still, I cannot help getting the feeling that the whole of any of the Bond books is this last showdown between Bond and the villain, and that there is a lot of flashy but meaningless motion between the point at which they first meet, and Bond realizes that the enemy will have to be extinguished, and the point at which he finally gets around to doing the job. The middle of these books is used for many subsidiary encounters between Bond and the villain, or Bond and the villain's henchman, but the incidents do not really lead into each other except in the most mechanical way. We rarely learn anything new about the villain in the interval, for he is obviously a bad actor to begin with. In the case of Mr. Big, we know all we need to know about his villainy from the stuff M and others feed to Bond at the start of the book. This is amply confirmed for Bond by his first encounter with Mr. Big.

Another weak point of Fleming's is logic. There is often no good reason for people in Fleming's books to do the things they do. In *Live and Let Die,* why does Bond come to New York in the first place, since the illicit coins are coming from the Caribbean and the assignment takes him directly to Florida after he has not accomplished anything in New York? The real reason is, of course, that Fleming wants to have a scene in Harlem, mainly to throw in some New York atmosphere, but this is far too apparent. Then, why does Bond leave for Florida on a train? Mr. Big is after him and it is clear that a train ride will give him a much better crack at Bond than a plane will, yet Bond takes the train. This kind of thing, while it creates incidents that are exciting, actually diminishes suspense, for if the hero keeps making wrong moves solely to create situations in which he is in danger, we do not believe that the danger is real; if it were, he would need all his resources in order to stay alive.

The incidents in Florida, while interesting in themselves, again add nothing to the total picture. This book takes the form of a detective story, but it is one in which the detective finds out nothing in the entire course of the narrative until the end of the book. True, Bond now knows that the robber's aquarium is the terminus in the States for the coins, but this does not effect in any way his final meeting with Mr. Big. That is the whole trouble with the book from the suspense point of view. Nothing in it effects the final encounter, there is no steady accumulation of knowledge with which the detective forces the villain into a corner and then battles it out with him. Bond might as well have been told everything at the outset, then gone to the island and fought it out with Mr. Big.

In *Moonraker,* Fleming avoids many of these objections, and it is a fairly well-plotted book, at least mechanically. One major objection, of course, is that neither Bond nor his cohort, Gala Brand, is able to figure out from the evidence what Hugo Drax is up to, and it is only Gala's chance discovery of Drax's notebook that tips things in their favor. But at least Bond is constantly trying to find out what is wrong about the Moonraker project, and the incidents along the way do create an atmosphere of suspicion. Still, there is one other curious incident from the point of view of plotting, and that is the famous bridge game at the start of the book. This incident is very well done, and there is definitely suspense created within the incident, but, of course, cheating at cards has nothing to do with plotting to destroy London. Also it might have been even more suspenseful if Hugo Drax had looked innocent when Bond went to work on the Moonraker instead of having had his reputation already blackened for the reader. One can argue the other side of this case—that the pattern of Drax's being guilty of a minor sin, then looking like a benefactor of England, and finally turning out to be a complete scoundrel is even more effective. It is still worth noting that Drax's cheating at cards is not necessary for the major plot, though I would insist that it is necessary for Fleming to have his villains do precisely this kind of thing.

Diamonds Are Forever is another random-incident-prone book. It starts promisingly with the scene on the African end of the smugglers' pipeline, then switches to M's telling Bond about things in London and ordering him to solve the riddle of where the diamonds are going to by taking over as a courier for the diamond syndicate. Bond completes this part of his assignment and is paid off by being told to bet on a horse at Saratoga. What happens in Saratoga is a nice little story about fixing the horses, but Bond's actions there have nothing to do with running down the pipeline. Then he goes to Nevada, gets in a fight with the Spang's hoods and destroys the whole gang, goes back to London on a ship, killing a couple of hoods on the way, and then finishes the diamond operation off by shooting down the other Spang brother as he hovers in a helicopter.

Bond's efforts at detection, here as elsewhere, come to very little. He finds out nothing that both he and the reader had not suspected from the beginning, and whatever he discovers, he finds not by sifting his way through a fog of

contradictory evidence, but by blundering his way into a
difficult position and then being informed by one of the
villains that he is at the other end of the line. Again, there
is nothing wrong with the individual incidents, and we often
wonder how each of them is going to turn out; it is just that
there is no continuity between the individual sub-adventures.

From Russia, with Love has, for Fleming, a simple, direct
plot line. SMERSH, at the start of the book, starts out to
kill Bond, and all their machinations are devoted to this end.
Some of the fights in Istanbul with Darko Kerim and the
gypsies may be extraneous, but there is at least some point
in having SMERSH try to get rid of him before they attack
Bond directly. There is a nice touch in the relaxation of
tension after the Russian agents on the Orient Express are
disposed of and before Red Grant appears. The same thing
happens when Grant dies and Bond goes on to face Rosa
Klebb.

Kingsley Amis, in his *James Bond Dossier,* argues that
there is little logic in this meeting of Bond and Klebb, but
here for once I think Fleming's plotting has the right feel
to it, logic to the contrary. It's only when you look back on
it that you notice the incongruity of Rosa's being so completely prepared to meet Bond, since she had no reason to
think Grant would fail, or that, even if he did, he would
give this rendezvous away to Bond. Amis makes a better
point when he says: "Rosa's novelties are not there to further
the plot (the book is nearly over anyway); they are the out-
ward signs of her nature, which is not only malignant and
ruthless, but devious, frighteningly inventive, rich in secret
and deadly skills. When we notice that she changes without
warning from a repulsive but feeble and harmless old woman

to a repulsive and active and lethal old woman, we know what we're dealing with. Room 204 was a witch's cell that day, just as Blofeld's Japanese establishment was an enchanter's castle. . . ."

Dr. No has virtues that few of Fleming's books possess. After the scenes in which Strangways is killed, Bond starts off by thinking he is on a dull assignment. Dr. No is only mentioned in passing in London, and it is only gradually that we realize the full scope of his activities. Once Bond and Quarrel arrive on Crab Key the plot is very direct, except that Honeychile, charming as she is, is added for a dash of piquancy, and has no real bearing on the combat between the bad doctor and Bond. The maneuvering before Crab Key is reached does go on a bit, but practically everything in the book relates to the central situation, which continually grows more menacing.

In *Goldfinger*, the plotting is extremely episodic. The big canasta game is followed by the big golf match, and neither of them have anything to do with the central situation of the novel, which indeed is not even disclosed until very late in the book. I think Fleming was at his best in describing gambling contests (and also underwater life), but it is often the case that creative people are apt to drag in what they do best, even when it has very little to do with what they are trying to create.

At any rate the long arm of coincidence is strained in this book. It seems rather odd that Goldfinger, who is reputedly one of SMERSH's big operators, never gets the idea that Bond may be spying on him, particularly since his cover story is that he is employed by Universal Export. Since SMERSH has a complete file on Fleming in *From Russia, with Love,* it is surprising that one of the their big men should know nothing about Universal. Even Kingsley Amis, who is prepared to accept this part of the tale, thinks it rather odd that Goldfinger doesn't dispatch Tilly Masterton, since there is no question that she is trying to avenge her sister.

The big Fort Knox robbery is also a little silly, I suppose, but I think most readers will go along with the gag, even though they may be somewhat fatigued by all the technical explanations of how the place was to be cracked. (This sort of thing is simply too intricate, and Fleming might have been well advised to heed his own strictures against overly complicated plans which the reader cannot follow.) But here, even the fight at the fort is not particularly gripping, although I did find myself wondering whether Bond's warning has been received, since Goldfinger has such massive forces at his disposal that Bond can't do much by himself and has to wait for the Marines (or whoever they are) to come to life and start blasting away at Goldfinger's allies. Perhaps this is why another fight, on the plane, is included, but again there is no particular logic to Goldfinger's kidnaping Bond. What with the episodic plotting and the dependence on the master villain's making rather bad errors in judgment, this book would have to be accounted one of Fleming's least suspenseful.

Thunderball, the first of the SPECTRE novels, starts off with what was by this time a typical Fleming ploy, Bond's chance encounter with the villain. This time it is an episode with a minor member of SPECTRE who is getting into shape at the same health-cure center as Bond. These episodes presumably make the later combat more personal for Bond and his enemies, but they are never satisfactorily connected to the plot. This is an unusually gratuitous encounter, since this particular villain is killed very early in the book, and Bond would have done precisely what he later does if he had never seen him.

Aside from this, there are several other incongruities. It is surely a little too convenient that the master criminals of SPECTRE don't know that Domino Vitali and Giuseppe Petacchi are brother and sister. Kingsley Amis points out that the best way to hide something is really to try to hide it and not to advertise its presence as SPECTRE does with the very conspicuous *Disco Volante*. It is my feeling that in a situation involving stolen atom bombs, nobody would worry about Largo and Company's legal rights and would move in once they had a fairly good idea of what was going on, or even a strong suspicion; of course, this would remove the chase at the end and the wonderful undersea fight. Still, the plot is simple, and if Bond plays some rather intricate games with Domino in order to win her over, he still seems to be keeping his eye on the ball most of the time.

The Spy Who Loved Me also has a nice, simple plot once Fleming gets around to it. The trouble is that better than half the book is a sort of young girl's confession of how bad men can be. Amis excuses this by saying that this is not really a Secret Service story, but I don't think this will do. I do not find, as he does, that the love life of Vivienne Michel is "treated with skill and imagination." I find its ponderously serious account of a young girl's love life weak and treacly and full of the endless tragedy of innocent Woman deserted by irresponsible Man. The trouble with this kind of story is not that it doesn't happen, but that it happens all the time, and for that very reason the most interesting perspective on these events is not that of a self-pitying female.

Once we get up in the Adirondacks with the hoodlums, we have some genuine terror, although it is of a kind that Fleming rarely handles. As Amis notes, the two hoods, minor members of a small-time gang, are hardly worthy opponents for the earth-shaking James Bond. The real problem is that the soap opera of Vivienne's memoirs has nothing to do with the sensational melodrama of her treatment by Horror and Sluggsy.

With *On Her Majesty's Secret Service,* we are back in the evil clutches of Blofeld and SPECTRE. The business with Tracy at the Casino and then the meeting with Draco is all very nicely done, but once again it has no effect on Bond's later encounter with Blofeld in the Alps. Of course, Draco and his men from the *Unione Corse* help Bond in the final roundup, but that's certainly because they are convenient. Bond's romance with Tracy at times intersects his conflict with Blofeld, but there is no integral connection between the two halves of the book.

Also, it is interesting that this master agent once again doesn't do what he sets out to do—to lure Blofeld from his sanctuary in Switzerland. In a tightly written book, we would not be started on false scents like this.

You Only Live Twice contains much extraneous data on Bond's mental condition at the beginning of the book, and then goes on to more disposable material, with Bond dickering with Tiger Tanaka for secrets and then being trained by Tiger to disguise himself as Japanese. Why he should have bothered trying to look Japanese is puzzling, since the minute he gets into Blofeld's poison garden he is in trouble anyway.

The poison garden gimmick is not convincing. Of course, all the villains' schemes in Fleming novels are fantastic, but with most of them we think that if such a thing were possible, it would be a profitable thing for a criminal or a spy to attempt. Blofeld's plot to increase the suicide rate is simply balmy.

The Man with the Golden Gun is very weak Fleming. Bond and the girl do not get together on a romantic or sexual level; Scaramanga turns out not to be a very good shot; and Amis notes that gimmicks are reworked from earlier books: the train from *Diamonds Are Forever* and the hoods' convention from *Goldfinger*. Fleming said he was having trouble working this one, and the plot is no more than adequate. Bond is sent to Jamaica to kill Scaramanga, and even the extraneous episodes until the final showdown sound tired. There is no reason why Bond and Scaramanga could not face each other at any point along the way, except that the final train ride makes a better setting for their shooting match.

The typical Fleming novel, then, has a beginning and an end but there is nothing much in the middle that necessarily takes us from one to the other. There is often excitement to the episodes in this middle part of the book, but these episodes rarely strengthen the tension implicit in the opposition of Bond and the villain. We never seem to feel in the course of one of these books that we are witnessing the operation of a well-adjusted machine or watching the growth of an increasingly fascinating organism from the few seeds present at the beginning. There is no sense of continuity to these books, no sense in which we feel that since X has happened, then Y must happen, which will in turn inevitably lead to Z. Without this kind of feeling, there can be no sense of urgency to the narrative and no suspense.

Still, Fleming must be doing something right, or can twenty million Englishmen be wrong? Fleming *is* doing something, something that people enjoy intensely. If a Fleming book lacks suspense, it has other qualities that make it unique. Fleming's books all unquestionably have an identity. If they are put together somewhat at random, still they are always put together in a certain way, so that the books, while very similar to each other in important respects, are rather different from those of other thriller writers.

It is my opinion that Fleming creates a consistent self-contained world which his readers can enter joyfully. (I am not talking about people who buy these books because Fleming is now vastly fashionable. It is beyond the limits of this work to speculate on why people of this sort read Fleming or go to discotheques or buy Beatles records. Also, I must admit, people who do anything merely because it is fashionable are either beyond my limited understanding or else far too scrutable.) This world has an identifiable landscape and a unique morality, and because of this, it is not important that the books lack suspense. People who like Fleming like becoming involved in the world of these books and are not after anything so superficial as the momentary tingles of suspense.

I particularly want to concentrate my attention on a certain pervasive relationship between Bond and the villains in these novels, but before doing that, it would be well to devote some further attention to Bond and his girls. There seems to be a widely held impression that there is only the crudest sort of sexual attraction between Bond and the various heroines, and that Fleming is a sort of pornographer. I have already stated that compared to other current writers in this genre, Fleming is not as preoccupied with sex as one might imagine from the publicity, and now I would add, following Kingsley Amis' lead, that what draws Bond to these women is not simply crude sex.

Amis makes the important point that all these women have "emotional baggage," and of a particular kind. All admittedly have gleaming physiques and, as Amis puts it, "fine, firm, faultless, splendid, etc. breasts," but it seems to me more important that beneath this very attractive facade, any Bond girl is "a defenceless child of nature, a wanderer in a hostile world, an orphan, a waif."

These girls have had many disagreeable experiences with men; most of them have no family, and the ones who start out by working for the villain find this occupation disagreeable. In other words, there is a certain degree of pathos to all these women; they are not merely sexual objects. I would think that it is essential to pornography that the women do not possess any moral or emotional attributes—they are purely and simply sex objects. Once a woman, no matter how attractive, has turned into a person, she has to be dealt with on a far more complicated basis than that of sex alone.

It seems to me that there is a puritanical streak in critics who assume that because a woman and a man at some point fall into bed the writer is a pornographer. I don't want to carry this to absurd lengths. There are certainly elements of wish-fulfillment in Bond's sexual adventures, but because the women are somewhat rounded characters with pasts and hopes for the future, there are also other elements present.

Finally, I would insist that the central concern of these novels is surely not in Bond's encounter with the girls, no matter whether you view these relationships as crudely sexual or as an expression of true love. Rather, the truly vivid relationship is that between Bond and the villains, and it is the villains, not the girls, who stand out in memory.

It has sometimes been observed that Ian Fleming's works are amoral. Bernard Bergonzi puts this case as well as anyone. He says: "What, briefly, emerges from Fleming's novels . . . is the total lack of any ethical frame of reference. It is all a question of *sensations,* more or less *fortes.* When Bond succeeds, it is not because Right is on his side, but simply because he is rather quicker on the draw, a little more handy with the throwing knife, just that much faster at lashing out with the steel-capped shoe. . . ."

Kingsley Amis, defending Fleming from this charge, replies: "I should have thought that a fairly orthodox moral system, vague perhaps but none the less recognizable through accumulation, pervades all Bond's adventures. Some things are regarded as good: loyalty, fortitude, a sense of responsibility, a readiness to regard one's safety, even one's life, as less important than the major interests of one's organization and one's country. Other things are regarded as bad: tyranny, readiness to inflict pain on the weak or helpless, the unscrupulous pursuit of money or power."

I think that Amis could find references in the novels to support his ethical contentions, but I think the dominant impression we have after reading any Fleming novel is that it is a question of sensations, not of moral choices. All the virtues listed by Amis are possessed as much by Fleming's super-villains like Dr. No and Hugo Drax (with the important difference that they don't possess a country to be loyal to) as they are by Bond.

This does not mean, however, that the Bond novels are lacking in morality, but merely that theirs is the morality of melodrama; someone has truly observed that in melodrama, the villain and the hero both want the money and the girl, and the only difference between them is the way in which they set about getting them. The situation in *The Spy Who Loved Me* is classic melodrama; both Bond and the villains are interested in Vivienne, and Bond shows his ethical superiority by being ever so much nicer about getting her.

Now, girls are not usually the object of contention in the Bond novels; in fact, many of the villains are completely uninterested in women. What matters is power. As Dr. No puts it: "That is why I am here. That is why you are here. That is why here exists." The particular form of power that matters most to both Bond and the villain, once the fight is joined, is the power of life and death—the power of one to kill the other. The villain is only different from Bond in that he is willing to kill many people, to attain limitless power, while Bond will be quite satisfied to kill the villain (and as many of his henchmen as happen to get in the way).

Of course, there is always a prelude to these fights. The villain has done so many nasty things in the past and will do more in the future unless he is stopped, but these larger ethical considerations are secondary in the personal fight to the death between Bond and the villain. When Amis lists tyranny as one of the things considered bad in Fleming's novels, he is being a little ingenuous. What is bad is the villain himself, and what is good is Bond himself—freedom of speech and the struggle against oppression don't enter into it.

The villain and Bond are not differentiated in the way they fight. Bond is no square; he does have some difficulty shooting a man in cold blood but once the fighting starts he gives as good as he gets. Bond often admires the "professionalism" of his opponents. Bernard Bergonzi has an interesting point to make about this: "And when SMERSH are succeeding . . . I have a strong suspicion that Mr. Fleming, on the imaginative plane, at least, admires them for it; for they succeed because they are *really* tough, more powerful than anyone else, more ready to get in and shoot first, more brilliantly ingenious in their methods. And, of course, quite unhampered by outworn ethical considerations."

So any moral superiority that Bond enjoys does not derive from his being slow on the draw. The real difference between Bond and the villains is that Bond is a handsome Englishman who handles easily all the paraphernalia of affluence, and the villains are all monstrous wogs who have made their money in trade. Kingsley Amis partially makes this point but does not carry it far enough. He says: "Throughout Bond's adventures no Englishman does anything bad. The villains are Americans, Bulgars, Chigroes, Corsicans, Germans, Italians, Jugoslavs, Koreans, Russians, Sicilians, Spanish-Americans and Turks. Goldfinger is theoretically British, but he holds a Nassavian passport and is really a displaced Balt. Red Grant has to be able to speak English like an Englishman so as to do his stuff as Captain Nash, but he comes from Ireland and had a German father. Sir Hugo Drax (national hero, Blades Club, life story in *Sun-*

day Express) looks a different case at first sight, but after minimal scratching he turns out to be a German called Hugo von der Drache, and a Graf too. So that's all right."

The villains are also monstrous-looking and/or have poor manners. The gambling scenes in *Goldfinger* and *Moonraker* are not strictly part of the plot; however, Goldfinger and Hugo Drax are cheats, and this is far more important in the moral universe of the Bond novels than their grandiose plans for killing large numbers of people. This proves, if one needed any further proof after looking at them, that they are not gentlemen, not one of us.

This is the real importance of all the conspicuous consumption that Bond engages in. In today's world, the mark of the gentleman is not that he has some fuddy-duddy set of ethics, but that he knows how to mix a proper martini, that he knows what brand of perfume his expensively accoutered girl friend is wearing, and that he enjoys his sports car. Today's gentleman has mastered the art of living, and he is with it. All this, of course, is not new with Fleming. Bergonzi quotes a passage from Hazlitt's "The Dandy School" (written in the 1820's) which reads: "You dip into an Essay or a Novel, and you may fancy yourself reading a collection of quack or fashionable advertisements; Macassar Oil, Eau de Cologne, Hock and Seltzer Water, Attar of Roses, *Pomade Divine* glance quickly through the page in inextricable confusion, and make your head giddy. Far from extending your sympathies, they are narrowed to a single point, the admiration of the folly, caprice, insolence, and affectation of a certain class. . . ."

All of Fleming's villains are outside this community of good manners and correct tastes. Many of them form a minority of one on the basis of looks alone. Dr. No has pincers instead of hands, contact lenses which he clicks metallically with his pincers; he has had his spine stretched by traction, has a completely bald skull, and looks like "a giant venomous worm wrapped in grey tin-foil." Mr. Big has "a great football of a head, twice the normal size and very nearly round." His skin is "grey-black, taut and shining like the face of a week-old corpse in the river." Hugo Drax has had his face redone by plastic surgery and the result has not been completely successful. His right ear "was not a perfect match with its companion on the left," and his right eye "had been a surgical failure. It was considerably larger than the left eye, because of a contraction of the borrowed skin used to rebuild the upper and lower eyelids, and it looked painfully bloodshot." Goldfinger is "out of proportion." He is short, "not more than five feet tall, and on top of the thick body and blunt, peasant legs was set, almost directly into the shoulders, a huge and it seemed exactly round head. It was as if Goldfinger had been put together with bits of other people's bodies. Nothing seemed to belong." A number of minor villains are similarly deformed.

When Tatiana first sees Rosa Klebb (*From Russia, with Love*) she is revolted by the smell of "cheap scent concealing animal odours." When Le Chiffre gets nervous playing *chemin de fer,* he sucks a benzedrine inhaler and a minor character informs us that he is a "filthy brute." The Spangs reek of the bad taste of quickly acquired American wealth. At first glance, Hugo Drax appears a "bullying, boorish, loud-mouthed vulgarian" to Bond.

Although many of Fleming's villains are extremely

wealthy, none of them have inherited their money. They have worked hard to obtain their ill-gotten wealth, and their origins are without exception lowly. Many of them have a grudge against society which made them feel like outcasts at a tender age. Scaramanga's pet elephant was killed by a policeman, which set him off on a life of crime. Hugo Drax was ugly even prior to plastic surgery, and the other boys at school were mean to him. Dr. No was tortured by his associates in a Chinese tong. Goldfinger was a refugee from Riga and started his business career in a pawnshop. Mr. Big, aside from his odd looks, is a Negro from Haiti who started life as a truck driver in Port-au-Prince. Ernst Blofeld wants more than anything in the world to be a French count.

In other words, James Bond is fighting for the life of an English gentleman against an assortment of ill-bred foreigners who want to destroy Bond's kind of life. For these ambitious *parvenus* have no thought of merely becoming part of the community which Bond represents. They would not know whether to have vodka made from potatoes or grain, and more important, they wouldn't care. The big villains are only interested in power, and Bond, except when he is trying to kill these villains, is merely trying to enjoy life and would never do anything so vulgar as to try and get ahead. The villains hate Bond because they can never be part of his world of easy consumption, and Bond returns their hatred, because he can't understand why these people are so wilfully different.

It is also interesting that it is the villains who are powerful and have massive organizations behind them. Bond is alone in his fight against this onslaught. Of course, he is a member of the Secret Service, but he rarely keeps M up to date on what he is doing. The feeling, even when he does have allies, is that they are weak mortals who may prove unreliable, while the villain has a perfect machine which has never made a mistake. There is a kind of decline-of-the-West aura to all this. The barbarians are strong, ruthless and organized, while Bond has been left to resist them and if he perishes nothing will stand in their way.

I think Fleming's feelings about the menace of this low breed of people are widely shared in the middle-class world today. In this country, people are alarmed by the civil rights movement when they find that some Negroes not only want to vote but actually want to live next door. The English middle class is menaced on many fronts. Something seems to have happened to the Empire, and the working-class people don't seem to know their place the way they used to. None of this can be directly expressed in an acceptable form among educated people. But if we can indulge ourselves in a world where all these different people are obviously villainous, we can work off a good deal of hostility, and this is precisely what the world of Ian Fleming offers.

Also, it is a relief to find that we don't have to have any exceptionally high ideals to be on the side of the angels. We merely have to feel, as Bond does, that these other queer people are the wrong sort and that they will never learn the art of gracious living which we have constructed from the pages of the glossy magazines. We are better than they are not only because we know our sports cars, but because they don't even realize what truly civilized values this knowledge represents.

For the world of consumership is not only the world of

James Bond, it is the world many of us live in for an important part of our lives. It is an alarming fact that people in the real world imitate those benighted souls who endlessly discuss on TV whether aspirin or Bufferin is quicker acting. Much small talk—and many people never talk anything else—is devoted to a comparison of tastes. Women are notorious for discussing what is in fashion, but men are also prone to wonder about their hi-fi sets, their cars, their tailors, and an endless variety of trinkets that assure their status. It is our way of assuring each other that we have something in common.

Once the middle-class world was securely bounded by a code of ethics and a set of manners. This was the way the world was in that Golden Age of all of us born and bred to the middle class in Edwardian England. This was the world of Ian Fleming's father, where a man knew what his duty was and did it. Today the code of the gentleman is sadly askew, and we are left nervously asserting our superiority because of the Sea Island shirts we wear.

Ian Fleming's books celebrate this world of consumption and its victory over the dangerous horde which menaces it in Asia and Africa and in the ghettos of our dark cities. Of course, not all the readers of Bond novels are assured English gentlemen moving easily among vodka martinis that are shaken, never stirred. But then neither were there many medieval kings in the audiences who were stirred by Shakespeare's *Henry V*. Works of fiction that celebrate a way of life are not addressed to those who are completely a part of the world being celebrated, but rather to those who are somewhat unsure of their right to be considered as members of the true faith. A man like James Bond, who always knew what he wanted and the way to possess it, would not find much satisfaction in the works of Ian Fleming. It is we poor souls who do not always dare face the monster, and often drink beer, and dine on leftovers, and have to wash the dishes after supper, who need reassuring.

Of course, this is all speculation, but I wonder if the life story of Ian Fleming does not somewhat support this line of reasoning.

Fleming came from an upper-class, Conservative family that was not remarkable for its wide range of sympathies for different kinds of people. Simon Raven, in discussing anti-Semitism in English public schools (Eton is a public school), said that it was of a mild kind and only had to do with the fact that English schoolboys were against anyone who looked or acted different, and that some Jews looked different. This animus seems to exist in Fleming's family, for Peter Fleming, in a book he wrote in 1934 (reprinted in 1956), in discussing the Soviet Union, said: "Outside the Kremlin, where a handful of men, presumably able and partly Jewish, control (on paper) the destinies of the far-flung Soviet Republics. . . ."

Further on in the same book, Peter Fleming writes an amusing little sketch about a discussion of Soviet drama. One of the characters is "Mr. Schultz, a very dapper Jew from Columbia University."

I'm not trying to say that these remarks by Peter Fleming were the fires that lit Hitler's ovens, but merely that in Ian Fleming's family, it was acceptable to point out that many people were different without any consideration for their feelings about the matter. It would not be surprising if Fleming felt somewhat the same way. Indeed, it is a very common English practice to consider the rest of the world as slightly wrong for not being more English.

Still, why should Ian Fleming's fantasy life have dwelt so much on this topic? Peter Fleming once wrote a suspense novel in which none of this was apparent. Ian Fleming was a successful man even before he wrote these novels. Why should he worry about such things?

Success came later to Ian Fleming than it does to some men. He did not go to Oxford; he turned down his commission after Sandhurst; he did not make a fortune in the City. It was only during the war that he came into his own, and even here he was mainly tied to a desk. Also, he came from a family that set very high standards. Peter wrote a number of books in the thirties that were very well received, and another brother, who today is head of a multimillion-dollar insurance group, had already started on his very successful career while Ian was still groping around.

He married late, and all his life he was careful about giving and receiving affection. Friends have commented that he had the habit of success, but for years he may have had more of the manner than the substance.

In other words, it is probable that Ian Fleming had certain doubts about himself. On the level of fantasy, these doubts expressed themselves in the extraordinary combats between someone vaguely like himself (Bond) and a number of villains who were representative of all those different people who made things difficult for him. This fantasy, which he was able to express very directly and powerfully, coincided with a similar fantasy of many other people who were unable to express it publicly.

I would insist more on my interpretation of the novels

than on these speculations about Fleming's psyche. I only include the latter because certain facts of his life do tend to support my thesis concerning his work.

If I am right, however, it is in a way fitting that out of fantasies nourished by doubts about himself came the unlimited success, the money, and the sure position in the world which he wanted. It is a rare man who is able to achieve his dreams by building on his nightmares.

DATE DUE

FEB 2 1			
MAR 1 0			
OCT 0 3 1980			
MAY - 8 1983			